P9-DBO-409

easy does it

CROSSWORDS

HARVEY ESTES

PUZZLE
WRIGHT
PRESS
New York

PUZZLE
WRIGHT
PRESS

New York

An Imprint of Sterling Publishing
387 Park Avenue South
New York, NY 10016

Puzzlewright Press and the distinctive Puzzlewright Press logo
are registered trademarks of Sterling Publishing Co., Inc.

The puzzles in this book originally appeared in the CrosSynergy Syndicate from 2003 to 2007.
Reprinted with permission

2 4 6 8 10 9 7 5 3 1

Published by Sterling Publishing Co., Inc.
387 Park Avenue South, New York, NY 10016
© 2011 by Harvey Estes
Distributed in Canada by Sterling Publishing
c/o Canadian Manda Group, 165 Dufferin Street
Toronto, Ontario, Canada M6K 3H6
Distributed in the United Kingdom by GMC Distribution Services
Castle Place, 166 High Street, Lewes, East Sussex, England BN7 1XU
Distributed in Australia by Capricorn Link (Australia) Pty. Ltd.
P.O. Box 704, Windsor, NSW 2756, Australia

Printed in China
All rights reserved

Sterling ISBN 978-1-4027-7417-1

For information about custom editions, special sales, premium and
corporate purchases, please contact Sterling Special Sales
Department at 800-805-5489 or specialsales@sterlingpublishing.com.

www.puzzlewright.com

CONTENTS

INTRODUCTION

I like to play around with words, and that's probably the main thing that got me hooked on making crossword puzzles. I think it's fun to knit words together into a puzzle grid (does that make me a "knit-wit"?) and try to work in as many interesting words and phrases as possible. And it's also enjoyable trying to come up with colorful and entertaining clues for the words that have been woven into the grid.

But the flavor and texture of a collection of crosswords mostly comes from the themes of the puzzles, which are the long answers that cause a puzzle to be about a particular thing. Here's a taste of what you'll find:

In puzzles like "Where Off" (p. 64) and "Article Rewritten" (p. 59), the theme answers are rather ordinary words ... but their clues give solvers an unusual way of looking at them. Puzzles like "Leaving Las Vegas" (p. 48) and "So to Speek" (p. 52) contain answers with words that get changed around a bit. This results in some familiar phrases that have a slightly different twist. Puzzles like "First of the Month" (p. 16) and "Myself and I" (p. 71) contain themes with answers that don't seem to have anything in common at first, but which hide a common element that emerges as you solve the puzzle. There are other types of themes that don't fit a category, but I hope each puzzle will, in its own way, provide you with a moment or two of entertainment and wordplay.

These puzzles are pretty easy, and I like that because it makes them accessible to everybody. If you like easy crosswords, this collection will probably suit you. But if you are an expert solver who likes more of a challenge, get out your stopwatch and challenge yourself to see how quickly you can finish each puzzle. That can help you get in shape if you want to compete in a crossword tournament!

The puzzles of this collection have never been published before on paper. I constructed them for online publication when I was a member of CrosSynergy, a group of some of the top puzzlemakers in the business. Many thanks to the members of CrosSynergy who helped me develop the themes, edit the clues, and fine-tune the grids. The puzzles are much better because of their efforts.

'Nuff said; get out your pencil or pen and start solving!

—Harvey Estes

INFLAMMATORY ENDING

ACROSS

1 Splendid display
5 Golfer's wheels
9 Seder cracker
14 Burden of proof
15 Allege as fact
16 "Suzanne" songwriter Leonard
17 The Bruins of the NCAA
18 Letter enc.
19 Stuff in a hot dog bun, briefly
20 "Don't beat around the bush"
23 Bugs or Erin
24 Stuff in a cell
25 Made privy to
28 Light beer
32 Redding of R&B
33 "Time in a Bottle" singer Jim
35 Scandal suffix
36 "Things won't change"
40 Lady's man
41 Current fashion
42 Tide type
43 Locust trees
45 Diplomat's building
48 "Wheel of Fortune" purchase
49 Boy Scout unit
50 "Cut me some slack ..."
56 Not exactly a genius
57 Cowardly visitor to Oz
58 Western defense gp.
59 "Be-Fudd-led" cartoon character
60 Crucifix inscription
61 Pretzel bag resealer
62 "___ you" (sneeze response)
63 Hawaii's state bird
64 Pianist Myra

DOWN

1 Wear a long face
2 Fairy tale opening
3 Consider, with "over"
4 Writer of Hebrew prayers
5 Havana honcho
6 Himalayan dangers
7 "Jurassic Park" bug trapper
8 Tough trip
9 His assassination made Roosevelt president
10 Vital vessels
11 Far East cuisine
12 Hellenic heaven honcho
13 Ottawa's prov.
21 Charged particle
22 Susan's "All My Children" role
25 "___ luck!"
26 Code of conduct
27 One over the Pope
28 Soldier's accessory of old
29 Short messages
30 First name in sewers
31 Grating
34 Stimpy's bud
37 Bugs Bunny, self-descriptively, and others
38 Get in shape
39 If need be
44 Brings about
46 Unification Church member
47 Fiddle stick
49 Strong string
50 School cheer
51 Treater's phrase
52 Lena of "Havana"
53 Fairy story
54 Inflammatory ending
55 Dips in gravy
56 Society newbie

1 P	2 O	3 M	4 P		5 C	6 A	7 R	8 T		9 M	10 A	11 T	12 Z	13 O
14 O	N	U	S		15 A	V	E	R		16 C	O	H	E	N
17 U	C	L	A		18 S	A	S	E		19 K	R	A	U	T
20 T	E	L	L	21 I	T	L	I	22 K	E	I	T	I	S
			23 M	O	R	A	N		24 R	N	A		
25 L	26 E	27 T	I	N	O	N		28 P	I	L	S	29 N	E	30 R	31
32 O	T	I	S		33 C	34 R	O	C	E		35 O	L	A
36 T	H	A	T	37 S	T	38 H	E	W	A	Y	39 I	T	I S
40 S	I	R		41 T	R	E	N	D		42 N	E	A	P
43 A	C	A	44 C	I	A	S		45 E	46 M	47 B	A	S	S	Y
			48 A	N	T		49 T	R	O	O	P		
	50 Y	51 O	U	K	N	52 O	W	H	O	W	53 I	54 T	55 I S
56 D	E	N	S	E		57 L	I	O	N		58 N	A	T	O
59 E	L	M	E	R		60 I	N	R	I		61 C	L	I	P
62 B	L	E	S	S		63 N	E	N	E		64 H	E	S	S

ANSWER, PAGE 79

7

FINDING NEMO

ACROSS

1 Went lickety-split
5 Make a pass at
10 Ending for auto or pluto
14 Glittery material
15 Sports stadium
16 ___ Hashanah
17 "Hang on ..."
20 Pivotal point
21 Homer's outburst
22 "___ Grows in Brooklyn"
23 Croatian capital
25 Stop worrying
27 Old White House nickname
28 Critic's pick
30 Make haste
31 Lao-___
32 Ivy League school, briefly
34 Sausage or city
37 Sculpture site near Atlanta
41 Backslide, medically
42 In a group of
44 Notre Dame's Parseghian
47 Survived, with "by"
48 Mork and ALF
50 Links letters
51 Charlie Chaplin's "The Great ___"
54 A Virgin Island
56 Octopus legs, e.g.
57 Palindromic plea
59 Send packing
60 It holds a microphone in a cradle
64 Windshield shading
65 Soothsayer
66 Rock outcropping
67 Lays eyes on
68 Starts doing business
69 Hockey's Phil, familiarly

DOWN

1 ___-mo replay
2 Flat breakfast items
3 No longer hidden
4 Take exception
5 Stage show-off
6 Mightily miffed
7 Drift
8 Like a bar owner's treat
9 Catch forty winks
10 Minotaur's land
11 React to with a guffaw
12 Put a value on
13 It may be given in a singles bar
18 Farm team
19 Not yet actualized
23 Compress, as a data file
24 Small curiosity
26 Official seals
29 Red purée
33 Post Office motto word
35 Take a bough?
36 Highway help org.
38 Cancel out
39 Ones who go foist?
40 Sip before the sack
43 Newsman Rather
44 Takes as one's own
45 Ron's "Happy Days" role
46 Play opener
49 Organ knob
52 Caterpillar constructions
53 Compact stuff
55 Power
58 Cold-cock
61 Chinese Chairman
62 Fourbaggers, in MLB
63 ___ trip

ANSWER, PAGE 80

CO-PILOTS

ACROSS

1 Excited like Miss Piggy?
8 Dessert style
15 South Seas islands
16 Seattle center fielder, e.g.
17 Pilot, perhaps
19 Cold War abbr.
20 Priced to move
21 Means justifiers, to some
22 Small German cars, for short
23 Swampy area
25 Type of engine
28 Thumbs-up vote
29 Deep cut
33 Crossword solvers' smudges
36 Once-divided city
38 Pilot, perhaps
40 Cooped up
41 Dorothy Gale lived with her
42 Reptilian "tail"
43 Tournament exemption
44 It's a gas in Canada
45 Trompe l'___ (visual deception)
47 Fallen Russian space station
49 Rick's old flame
53 Made into a lariat
55 "How about a ___?"
58 Pilot, perhaps
61 The Fab Four
62 King with 700 wives
63 Baby's room
64 Song from "Jesus Christ Superstar"

DOWN

1 Bounces like a bunny
2 Phil of folk music
3 Reverse or first
4 Like a pale face
5 Trailing behind
6 Elsa and Simba
7 Makes, as lakes
8 Pilot Earhart
9 "See ya!"
10 Comics bark
11 Roger Bannister's distance
12 "Door's open, come ___"
13 Title document
14 Makes mistakes
18 "Fire and Rain" singer
22 Hindu deity
24 Discharge
25 Fab Four flick
26 Great Lake tribesmen
27 Carta starter
28 It may burn a hole in one's kimono pocket
30 More affected
31 Some plums
32 Busy places
34 In ___ (not yet born)
35 Disencumber
36 "___-Hur"
37 Film fish
39 Cry companion
43 Specimen for the lab
46 Fictional Gantry
47 Copycat's cry
48 Ruben Studdard and Kelly Clarkson, for example
49 Barnes & Noble ID
50 Place
51 The Sun, for one
52 Drama divisions
54 Fancy-schmancy
55 Song about Him
56 Well-informed about
57 Rowlands of "Hope Floats"
59 Chihuahua cheer
60 Ode title opener

ANSWER, PAGE 83

9

WHATSA MATTER?

ACROSS

1 Amontillado container, for Poe
5 Part of a dying fire
10 Slugger Sammy
14 Go backpacking
15 "Grease" singer Frankie
16 ___-a-porter
17 The Emerald Isle
18 "Ready or not, here ___!"
19 Down-to-earth
20 Well-chosen
21 Send Abzug to college?
23 Pauses for pocket bread?
25 Positive replies
26 Say "y'all," say
27 Leave in the lurch
28 Narrow victory margin
29 Egg carton rating
33 Counterpart to Kitt's evil twin?
38 Repelled or reproduced
39 Celeste or Ian
41 Ethically neutral
45 Home of the Buccaneers
46 Pew-warmer's position
47 Smart clothing?
51 Mediterranean booze?
53 Bio. or chem., e.g.
54 Taking care of business
55 Done to ___
56 Wash cycle
57 Chinese prefix
58 Correct but unlikely reply to "Who's there?"
59 Fish in a melt
60 Freshman, probably
61 Like shakers and movers
62 Baseball great Slaughter

DOWN

1 Make tawdry
2 Plane person
3 Easily startled
4 Barbie's new fiancé
5 Throw out in the street
6 Chest-thumping
7 Ball hit just over the infield
8 Red Muppet dolls
9 Cambodian currency
10 Indulgent spells
11 "Otherwise, you won't like it!"
12 Paint basecoat
13 Waiting room cry after "Next!"
21 U-turn from NNW
22 Without sheet music
24 Ending with chick
27 Like many who sign
29 Shout dreaded by the defense
30 Political commentator Reagan
31 Fuss and bother
32 OED offering: Abbr.
34 Non ___ (unwelcome)
35 Become less reserved
36 Folksy
37 "Insomnia" star
40 Boat basins
41 Not more than
42 Nasty sort
43 Connected to the Web
44 Gymnast Mary Lou
45 Paving goo
47 Walter, who had a secret life
48 Provide with gear
49 Drink slowly
50 Actress Braga of "Kiss of the Spider Woman"
52 Café lightener
56 Sault ___ Marie

ANSWER, PAGE 84

HE PLAYED GOD ...

ACROSS

1 Jacob's first wife
5 ERA, e.g.
9 Talks with one's hands
14 Earthenware pot
15 "Les Misérables" author
16 Commotion
17 Last word before the first bite, perhaps
18 Word on a map of Uzbekistan
19 Not quite erect
20 ... in "Bruce Almighty" (2003)
23 Where a farmer's ears may be attached
24 Emulate Gregory Hines
25 Stroke gently
28 Jerk, as a knee
31 Stick together
33 Comedian DeLuise

36 ... in "Skidoo" (1968)
38 1847 Melville novel
40 AC measure
41 Sean Connery, for one
42 ... in "Oh, God!" (1977)
47 Some commuter trains
48 Destitute
49 Knocks for a loop
51 Anka's "___ Beso"
52 Server's reward
54 Tries to lose
57 ... in "The Seven Deadly Sins" (1992)
62 Place for cards or coffee
64 Bossy bellows

65 Canal of Sal, in song
66 Set straight
67 Coup d'___
68 Finishes an i
69 Bother terribly
70 They catch acrobats, on a bad day
71 Farm females

DOWN

1 Good earth
2 St. ___ fire
3 Red state?
4 Shelter for an airplane
5 Sitarist Ravi
6 Gang's territory
7 Thickening agent
8 Sign from a landlord
9 Movie sequel to "Hair"?

10 Tiny bit
11 Depart serenely
12 Islanders' org.
13 Obeyed "Down in front!"
21 Shake or break follower
22 Per capita
26 Flamboyant Flynn
27 Readings during worship services
29 Tommy Lee Jones baseball film
30 "Swan Lake" attire
32 Pensive sounds
33 Motherless calf
34 Broken mirror and others
35 Part of an Apollo path
37 Terse

39 Tram filler
43 Bart Simpson exclamation
44 TV entertainer Adams
45 They exert the right to bare arms ... and more
46 Hissy fit
50 Leave, like Louisiana once did
53 Spin doctors, often
55 Dice roll
56 High-end hotel option
58 One of Chekhov's "Three Sisters"
59 Shopping convenience
60 Watery ditch
61 Military meal
62 ___ kwon do
63 The Crimson Tide's st.

ANSWER, PAGE 87

ONE OF THE MAGNIFICENT SEVEN

ACROSS

1 Häagen-___ ice cream
5 Move off quickly
10 Pronto on "ER"
14 Mars: Prefix
15 Single-handed
16 The life of Riley
17 1967 movie of 39-Across, with "The"
19 Allies' foe
20 Hello from Ho
21 Movie series of 39-Across
23 Prefix with drama
25 For whom the bell tolls, per Donne
26 Put away
30 Does foundry work
34 Irish tongue
35 Buckeye State
37 Be gaga over
38 Part of a drumbeat
39 Charles of "The Magnificent Seven"
41 Contend
42 Use the olfactories
44 Word before skirt or hoop
45 Sweat drop
46 Sawing logs
48 ___ stove
50 Pianist Peter
52 In fine fettle
53 1965 movie of 39-Across, with "The"
58 Montana metropolis
61 Years ago
62 1974 movie of 39-Across
64 Cold feet
65 Baseball great Satchel
66 "Is this the right place?"
67 "Jabberwocky" opener
68 Tiniest bit
69 Steamed up

DOWN

1 One of baby's first words
2 Seed cover
3 Star of "The Producers"
4 "And that's that!"
5 Singing the blues
6 Dirt clump
7 Move like molasses
8 ___ a time
9 Dimes, to dollars
10 Iodine source
11 Prepare to take off
12 Warts and all
13 New Age musician John
18 Cornell rival
22 Macho dude
24 "Phew!" inducer
26 ___ date (makes wedding plans)
27 Coal haulers
28 "Looks like trouble"
29 Prepare to hem
31 Romantic writing
32 "The Practice" event
33 Like a sesame bagel
36 Norse port
39 The sound of censorship
40 Scout's recitation
43 They may charge interest
45 John of "The Blues Brothers"
47 Dresses with care
49 Porker in pictures
51 Daytime talk show host from 1986 to 2011
53 Like some C's
54 De novo
55 March tourney sponsor
56 Islamic leader
57 Raise Cain
59 Brit's wheel
60 Barely made, with "out"
63 Nickname on "The West Wing"

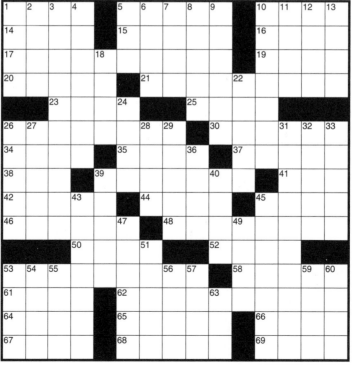

ANSWER, PAGE 88

GOT M-I-L-K?

ACROSS

1 Dieter's measure
8 Having a stiff upper lip
15 "I don't want to hear it!"
16 Large fleet of planes
17 EM
19 "Cut it out!"
20 Kevin Bacon, in "Footloose"
21 Turn right
22 Card with a single pip
24 Fork over
25 Matthew of "Friends"
27 EYE
32 Supply of arms
33 ER personnel
34 Some ER cases
35 16, in ancient Rome
36 U.S. soldiers, in 1917: Abbr.
38 Nabokov title heroine
41 Shipping magnate Onassis, briefly
43 Reproduced word for word
47 ELLE
50 Mike or Cicely
51 Type of discrimination
52 Kenny G's instrument
53 "Fantasia" frame
54 Meeting gp.
55 Off-white
58 KAY
63 Most bohemian
64 Duty-free time
65 Having a will
66 "Popeye" cartoon kid

DOWN

1 J.E.B. Stuart's country
2 "The Simpsons" storekeeper
3 Van Buren's sister
4 "... ___ put it another way ..."
5 Bridle strap
6 "Haven't ___ you somewhere before?"
7 Fair-hiring letters
8 Visibly woeful
9 Common noun suffix
10 Bobby of hockey
11 "Cymbeline" heroine
12 Wait on hand and foot
13 Stuck
14 Not of the cloth
18 "The Nanny" portrayer Drescher
22 Palindromic cry
23 Dirty dog
24 Compadre
25 100 centimos
26 Soph. and jr.
28 Reed or Stout
29 For naught
30 Nile city
31 Diet guru Jenny
37 Brimless hat
38 Toward the stern
39 Employee benefit, perhaps
40 Gives in
42 Like lower tuition
43 Left Coast airport, for short
44 Revolts
45 Santa ___, California
46 Gene's "Superman" role
48 "Not so fast!"
49 Anthropologist Margaret
54 Pain in the neck
55 Cook up
56 "The Grapes of Wrath" extra
57 Wall Street letters
58 Move, as an eyelash
59 Ewe's milieu
60 Golfer Ernie
61 Before, in verse
62 "Prêt-à-Porter" actor Stephen

ANSWER, PAGE 91

13

FIVE SIMPLE WAYS TO REMEMBER JOHN RITTER

ACROSS

1 Corned beef concoction
5 Top-drawer
9 Shutterbug's setting
14 Skillful
15 Fork over, with "up"
16 Still in contention
17 Baked potato topper
19 March of ___
20 Documentary hosted by Ritter
22 Wolfe of fiction
23 Slangy assent
24 Wacko
25 Witchy women
27 Bo Derek flick
28 Military operations center
31 Composer of fugue fame
34 Some Wharton grads
37 One of the Chipmunks
38 Farm division
39 Ritter's "___ Simple Rules for Dating My Teenage Daughter"
41 Dynamic prefix
42 Dumbstruck
44 Place for a small house
45 Carey or Barrymore
46 "A Perfect Spy" author
48 Enzyme ending
50 "Twittering Machine" painter
51 Where to look, in "Misty"
53 Tom Brokaw's employer, once
56 Appointment
58 Series for which Ritter was nominated for an Emmy
61 Character of a culture
63 Nervous
64 Make up (for)
65 Swim competition
66 Commotion
67 Much, slangily
68 Fiery heap
69 Half a pair of footwear

DOWN

1 Rash
2 Partner of beyond
3 Imbibe impolitely
4 Damsel's deliverer
5 "Sorry"
6 ___ a customer
7 Like a moonscape
8 Prefix with sphere
9 Mood rings or pet rocks, e.g.
10 Billy Bob Thornton movie with Ritter
11 Chore shortcut
12 Walkie-talkie word
13 Cancún coin
18 Bake sale order
21 Frat letter
26 Altar constellation
27 1972 small screen series with Ritter
28 Queens stadium name
29 Stable parent
30 Sufficiently, in poetry
31 Rescue, with "out"
32 Dermal dilemma
33 Expert gunner
35 Hurt the dentist, perhaps
36 Cabinet dept.
40 One Patriot to another
43 Palindromic preposition
47 Stephen of "V for Vendetta"
49 Faction
51 Bowler's hangout
52 Part of MTM
53 "Cool!"
54 Rudimentary
55 Court assistant
56 Burst of laughter
57 Palindromic comics dog
59 Like a Dalí watch
60 Porgy's partner
62 Wave carrier

ANSWER, PAGE 92

CRAZY PEOPLE ARE WHAT THEY EAT

ACROSS

1 See eye to eye
5 Give out
9 The whole spectrum
13 Haley or Trebek
14 Truth alternative
15 Bangkok tongue
16 Get in return
17 Involved with
18 Break in relations
19 They rule the roost
22 Distant relative of Scopes?
24 Current named for the infant Jesus
25 Mexican month
28 ___ Clemente
29 Doesn't keep a poker face
30 Dictator Amin
31 Universal donor
33 With 32-Down, 2002 British Open champ
35 They eat nutritious stuff
40 Subway Series team
41 Town on the Thames
42 Proofreader's "let it stand"
43 Lenten symbol
44 Veteran
46 Childcare writer LeShan
47 Punching tool
48 Lobe locale
50 They rob strongboxes
56 Tug of war cry
57 Cougar or Mustang, e.g.
58 Provide a chair for
60 Name on an old column
61 Romanov ruler
62 Peace of mind
63 Gusto
64 E-mail command
65 Tall dinosaur, for short

DOWN

1 Cookie container
2 Seine sight
3 Well-worn way
4 Montreal baseballer
5 Safe to swallow
6 Lackadaisical response
7 Like calling telemarketers at home
8 Lucy Ricardo, to Ethel Mertz
9 Blade brand
10 Right now
11 Clumsy fellow
12 Teen woe
20 Reform Party candidate
21 Snooped (around)
22 Inhaler target
23 Bread recipients
26 Made corrections to
27 Sonora snooze
32 See 33-Across
34 ICU staffers
36 WWII fighter planes
37 Big name in bouquets
38 Caveman of comics
39 In the books
44 Run a tab
45 Wood furniture makers would buy
47 G-sharp equivalent
49 Bowling alley button
50 "You bet!"
51 Donations for the destitute
52 Trojan horse, e.g.
53 ___ all-time high
54 Area away from the battle
55 Enclosure with a ms.
56 Dispensable candy
59 John Ritter's father

ANSWER, PAGE 95

15

FIRST OF THE MONTH

ACROSS

1 Florida city, informally
5 Messing around the "Will & Grace" set
10 Pt. of SASEs
14 "I missed the birdie putt, but made ___"
15 "In other words ..."
16 Computer option list
17 The grass is always greener over this, for Erma Bombeck
19 Software purchaser
20 Railroad locomotives
21 Egypt and Syr., once
23 Cable ch. for old films
24 VCR button pushed for a snack break
25 Gathering after hitting the slopes
27 "___ it the truth!"
28 Mil. sub division?
30 Axis foes
31 52-wk. periods
32 Three-note chord
34 "Biography" network
35 Monkey bars
37 Therapeutic center, for short
40 Ditties for the deity
41 Dye container
44 Seventh planet from the sun
46 Biscuit, to the gravy
47 Baylor University site
48 Long story writer
50 Digital hour and minute separator
51 Verb ender, in England
52 List shortener, for short
53 In general
55 Totenberg of NPR
57 What the months abbreviated in 17-, 25-, 35-, and 48-Across have in common
59 Hit the horn
60 Overdo it onstage
61 Assassination accusation
62 Being broadcast via idiot box
63 City on the Seine
64 Like one end of a pool

DOWN

1 Wages, excluding overtime
2 In the outdoors
3 Toy pistols
4 Painter who may take months to do a wall
5 Cubes with spots
6 Ambulance personnel, for short
7 Arthur who played female roles
8 Incurred, as debts
9 Capital of Turkey
10 Turkey alternative, in some cuisine
11 Takes for a home, perhaps
12 Like some sweaters
13 Conjecture
18 Pitched a whole step above the key of D
22 Races with hand-offs
25 Market watcher
26 Sound right after an angry exit
28 Java lovers gather around it
29 Nonverbal "Alas!"
32 Capillary's cousin
33 Test-driver's car
35 Eyre of distinction
36 Econ. yardstick
37 Meet by chance
38 Shoreline problem
39 One without wealth
41 Get an appraisal for
42 Altar boy
43 Gets in shape
45 Facilitator of a night out for parents
47 Phrased
49 Chump
50 Small island
53 Comedian Johnson
54 British submachine gun
56 Off-road transport, briefly
58 Debtor's note

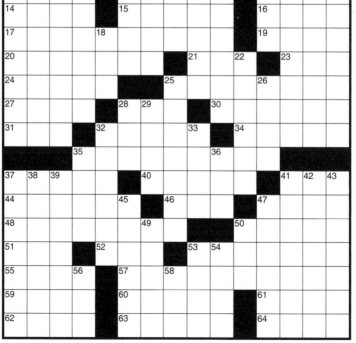

ANSWER, PAGE 96

MICKEY MOUSE BREAKS DOWN

ACROSS

1 None at all
8 Amp toters
15 Greed
16 Extra numbers
17 MIC
19 NFL 6-pointers
20 Jacob of journalism
21 Reserve
24 Celt or Highlander, e.g.
25 "Um, pardon me ..."
29 KEY
32 From ___ Z
33 Selects, with "for"
34 Male model Lanzoni
35 Sharp-tasting
38 Trip to the plate
39 Went for
40 Duke's st.

43 AFL's other half
45 MO
49 ___ oneself (do without)
50 List shortener
51 Bonn's river
52 Will beneficiary
53 "Exodus" role
54 USE
62 Romans, for one
63 Tax-sheltered nest egg
64 Batman and Robin, to Riddler
65 Piled up

DOWN

1 Rebel Turner
2 Female cells
3 Keg outlet
4 First name in soul
5 Commanded

6 Cold desserts
7 Gumshoe, for short
8 Cameo carvings
9 Tip of the House, of old
10 Gets off the fence
11 It comes before com
12 Wilde country: Abbr.
13 Profit ender
14 Snake's warning
18 Oscar Mayer's parent company
21 Spy org.
22 He danced in "Silk Stockings"
23 Punch a timecard
24 Republicans, for short
25 Speedy steed

26 Japanese cooker
27 Newspaper issue
28 Red Book author
30 The Pentagon is its HQ
31 Time and again
36 Big name in cognac
37 First name in Ugandan infamy
38 Chair part
39 Kind of PC monitor
40 The restless ones, in a cliché
41 Bow of silents
42 Silent communication: Abbr.
44 Poem of Sappho
46 Poke fun at

47 List of missed mistakes
48 Chicken servings
52 Bald spot hiders
53 Smallest amount of gold?
54 Half a score
55 King Kong, for one
56 Basinger of "L.A. Confidential"
57 Language ending
58 Gun lobby org.
59 Frozen water, in Wittenberg
60 Lode contents
61 Hula hoop, e.g.

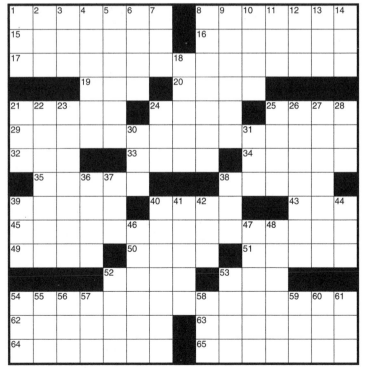

ANSWER, PAGE 81

17

A HATFIELD WHO WAS THE REAL MCCOY

ACROSS

1 Letters on an old map of Asia
5 Book of maps
10 Steelworkers smelt them
14 Tiny biter
15 "All in the Family" spin-off
16 When tripled, a war film title
17 Correct the spelling of, e.g.
19 Spelling on television
20 With 29-Across, a Righteous Brothers song
22 Michael, to Kirk
23 "You ___ for it!"
24 Thumbs-up
25 Big occasion
27 No and J, e.g.
29 See 20-Across
30 Telly network
33 Concert cry
37 Fifth-century pope
38 Piglet's pal

39 With 59-Across, a Righteous Brothers song
41 Jean-___ Picard
42 Travelers' stopovers
44 Uncomfortable underclothing condition
45 Sound of disapproval
46 Bobby Hatfield's Righteous Brothers partner Bill
48 Trains overhead
50 Real bargain
51 IRS review: Abbr.
54 Petty quarrels
58 Sardine holder
59 See 39-Across

62 Roughly
64 Music for "Aida," e.g.
65 ___-do-well
66 Basic belief
67 Most eligible, to the SSS
68 Small whirlpool
69 Conductor Previn
70 Halloween costume part

DOWN

1 Eclipse shadow
2 Rural "skyline"
3 In a rut
4 Offended olfactorily
5 Pastor's "You can go home now"

6 "Driving Miss Daisy" Oscar winner Jessica
7 "Filthy" money
8 Chihuahua "ciao"
9 Turn traitor, with "out"
10 Baseball's "Master Melvin"
11 U.N. delegate Eleanor
12 Off the mark
13 Father Christmas
18 Fathers, to Felipe
21 Washington College president Robert E. ___
26 Kilmer of "The Doors"
28 Pure white

29 Big name in skating
30 Material for a fiery sermon?
31 All tuckered out
32 Like dew
34 Stage signal
35 Familiar, as friends
36 Poor periodical
40 Triangles in the "Odyssey"
43 Hearst kidnapping gp.
47 Dubya, as a collegian
49 "Will & Grace" or "Ellen," e.g.
51 Forest quaker
52 Turn over
53 More urgent
55 Singer Apple
56 Links cries
57 Quarterback's play
60 Bene beginning
61 Word after going or flat
63 Kid of jazz

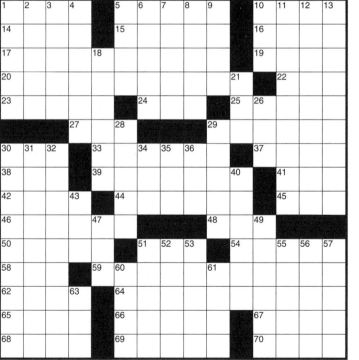

ANSWER, PAGE 82

TIGHTEN YOUR BELT

ACROSS

1 Joe of "My Cousin Vinny"
6 Gob of gunk
10 What weightlifters count
14 John of "Tommy"
15 Margarita flavoring
16 Taxiing place near Paris
17 Try this first
18 Ballerina Pavlova
19 Muffin type
20 Cher child of 1969
23 Serve well
26 Executed perfectly, as a dismount
27 Ancient Greek seer
28 Pacific coast country
30 Harmless slitherer
32 Opposite of NNW
35 Puts to work
36 Cyberspace initials
37 Jack and Jill's vessel
38 Part of the school yr.
39 Spun sugar
43 Transplant taker
44 Flip chart holders
45 Fire remnants
48 Yellow ribbon site
49 One well-versed in verses
52 Louver part
53 First-class
54 Word before trail or route
58 Scat artist Fitzgerald
59 Jack-o'-lantern feature
60 Barcelona buddy
61 Guitarist Lofgren
62 Really likes, with "up"
63 Kissinger's boss, once

DOWN

1 Get-up-and-go
2 Right angle
3 RR terminus
4 Cooks up
5 Lacking lettuce
6 Less than thrilled
7 Dryer refuse
8 Former Atlanta arena
9 Cool cat
10 Pop singer Dupree
11 Robin Hood portrayer Flynn
12 Shop class tool
13 Church council
21 Say with conviction
22 Lock producer
23 Like a slug
24 Do blackboard duty
25 Eunuch's charge
28 Equivalent of twenty fins
29 Christmas play prop
31 Fill to the gills
32 Less loony
33 Inch furtively
34 "Family Ties" mother
37 Rye partner
39 Apple leftover
40 Treading the boards
41 Minimal tide
42 Bakery container
43 River mouths
45 Sitcom hillbilly with Baer and Ryan
46 ___ Vanilli of lip-sync fame
47 Hoops
48 Future indicators
50 Tijuana time
51 Part of ICU
55 Snaps
56 "I" problem
57 "A Beautiful Mind" director Howard

ANSWER, PAGE 85

HOLY MEN, HOLEY TEETH

ACROSS

1 "Understood"
6 Model makers' purchases
10 Get rid of a watermelon seed, e.g.
14 Cockamamie
15 Memo starter
16 Top-flight
17 Gathering point
18 Pack away
19 "You've Got Mail" director Ephron
20 Spiritualists
22 Trip of much travail
23 Some urban railways
24 Wile E. Coyote's mail-order company
25 Photo finish?
26 Napoleon's second exile isle

29 Carney or Garfunkel
30 Has an evening meal
33 Don Juan's mom
34 "Quiet on the ___!"
35 With 55-Across, what the 20-Across do when forgoing Novocain?
40 Double curve
41 Leafy veggie
42 Gala gathering
43 Butter portion
44 Remembered for all time
48 Not quite right
50 Eden event
51 What Noah saved for a rainy day?
54 Make, as a putt

55 See 35-Across
58 Swenson of "Benson"
59 Cross to bear
60 Move laterally
61 "Act now!"
62 Eight bits
63 Mournful peal
64 Fishing eagle
65 "___ who?"
66 Admirable quality

DOWN

1 Two-inch putt, for one
2 Shaquille of the NBA
3 Dashboard instruments, briefly
4 Machu Picchu builder
5 Cause anguish to

6 Osculation invitation to Kate
7 While doing one's job
8 Captain Picard's counselor
9 Uses a Singer
10 Rooftop visitor, some believe
11 Bad judgment in social situations
12 Withdrawing
13 Boiler that may whistle
21 Egotist's focus, in Essen
25 Rat's learning place
26 Tax form ID
27 Pull the plug on
28 Flanders of "The Simpsons"
30 Clear the way

31 Constellation of Polaris
32 Adding to the scrapbook, e.g.
36 Hits the slopes
37 Helmet add-on for TV
38 Shade tree
39 Org. of Eagles and Cardinals
45 Rewards from the boss
46 Gentle letters
47 49th state
49 Go round the rink
51 Hospital helpers
52 Esther of "Good Times"
53 Prepared to propose
55 Disorderly crowds
56 Single-named Irish singer
57 Coventry containers

ANSWER, PAGE 86

ART OF COMEDY

ACROSS
1 Prefix with science
5 Michael's "Mr. Mom" costar
9 Blackjack request
14 Wander widely
15 Pizzeria appliance
16 Singer with hip-sync?
17 Off-rd. transports
18 Omar's "Mod Squad" character
19 Storytellers
20 Art Carney Broadway play
23 Long swimmer
24 Go bad
25 Road warning
26 1988 Hanks film
29 Stop by
31 Community school org.
32 Warrior princess of TV
33 Charlotte of "The Facts of Life"
34 Any minute now
35 Chows down
36 Art Carney Oscar movie
39 Knock on the noggin
40 Whirling water
41 Phone bk. listings
42 Method of meditation
43 GPs and OBs
44 Video store transaction
47 Barely get, with "out"
48 Neth. neighbor
49 Years and years
50 Spectrum part
51 Art Carney television show, with "The"
54 Big name in copying
57 Meadow sounds
58 Aphrodite's son
59 "Dave" star Kevin
60 Made a touchdown
61 Silver suffix
62 Wabbit wival
63 Comes together
64 Go a few rounds

DOWN
1 Took to the stump
2 May honoree
3 Fruit with an "outie"
4 "___ sorry!"
5 Blabbed about
6 Force off the premises
7 Ashcroft's predecessor
8 Held by the heat
9 "___, ball" (Norton's "address the ball" line)
10 Rival of Bjorn
11 Govt. dam builder
12 Russian commune
13 Superman's insignia
21 Moisture remover
22 Factory
26 Is acquitted, slangily
27 Keen on
28 Speeders step on it
30 Hooded jacket
31 Polliwogs' places
32 Television tube filler
34 Western carryall
36 Wendy's kidnapper
37 Mocha's country
38 Bridge bid, briefly
39 "See ya!"
44 Parrot perches
45 Dawn deity
46 Second-rate
48 Ali, e.g.
49 Online letters
51 Fine-tune
52 Eli's school
53 Part of CNN
54 Jaguar model
55 Pipe part
56 Where the net hangs

ANSWER, PAGE 89

NATIONAL BORDERS

ACROSS

1 They have little to wag
9 Dilapidated dwellings
15 Military incursion
16 Bathhouse
17 Crimson cup caches?
19 Floppy
20 Color bearers for artists
21 TV hubby of Phyllis
25 Transport up to the Enterprise
26 Isle of exile
30 Type of drug for infections
34 "We ___ the World"
35 Woodwind player
38 Part of a U.
39 Rehab filming session?
42 Bigger than big
43 Treeless tract
44 World War II battle site, for short
45 Distant balls of gas
47 Viewing audience estimates
49 Church niche
52 Up to the task
53 Tchaikovsky ballet
57 Pt. of PGA
61 Actor trying to do chin-ups?
65 Purpose
66 Lives it up
67 Must
68 Homer or Dante

DOWN

1 Wren or hen, e.g.
2 "That's ___ haven't heard"
3 Briefs, briefly
4 Set your mind to
5 Word with Wednesday
6 Midafternoon, on a sundial
7 Chilling Chaney
8 Buckle alternative
9 Word before model
10 ___ corpus
11 Somewhat over the top
12 Defeatist's word
13 Joint where kids sit
14 Exams for srs.
18 Truck compartment
22 What little things mean, in song
23 Picture puzzle
24 Laugh derisively
26 Goldman's business partner
27 Rainbow-colored fish
28 Andrew Wyeth subject
29 "Idol" star Clay
31 Sarge's superior
32 Gone by air
33 Treble clef readers
36 Drawing in brown
37 Category for laid-back people
40 Nuts
41 Wall Street bear's order
46 Broken-bone stabilizer
48 Make airtight
50 ___ Domingo
51 Hosp. readout
53 Place for a guard
54 Drop off
55 Initial stake
56 Behold, to Brutus
58 Fair to middling
59 Popeye's ___ 'Pea
60 Arbor abode
62 WWII general ___ Arnold
63 Former Bush spokesman Fleischer
64 ER figure

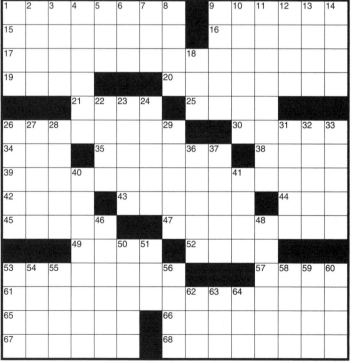

ANSWER, PAGE 90

PASS THE TATERS

ACROSS

1 Pesto flavoring
6 Stylish
10 Detective's assignment
14 Entreaty to "all ye faithful"
15 Model T, e.g.
16 Too stylish
17 Tater
20 Part of HMS
21 Resemble, with "after"
22 Sesame seed paste
23 Hoods for monks
25 Throat drop
26 A single stroke under par
28 Characteristic carriers
29 Opted for home cooking
30 Gravy holder
31 Sticky stuff
34 Tater
38 Common street name
39 Wild party
40 Wipe out
41 Measuring device
43 Passes out
44 Explorer or university
47 Schlepped
48 Some bellybuttons
49 Righthander Hershiser
50 Clumsy hand
53 Tater
56 Fishy yarn?
57 Anise-flavored liqueur
58 Heaps
59 Belgian river
60 1982 cyberflick
61 Play matchmaker for

DOWN

1 "Oh, bother!"
2 Bothersome spots
3 Chives partner
4 Global gold gp.
5 Radical liberal faction
6 Wine containers
7 Cronyn of "Cocoon"
8 "Is ___?" (Last Supper question)
9 Start liking
10 Redeems, with "in"
11 "Catch-22" star Alan
12 Redford/Newman flick, with "The"
13 Vocalist Gorme
18 Ivy League member
19 Cause of low visibility
24 Norse war deity
25 Vermont senator Patrick
26 Bag of diamonds
27 "___ cost you"
28 Pig out
30 Victor at the keyboard
31 International car race
32 Drum out
33 Scores for free throws
35 Free throw
36 Pop singer named for an entree
37 Pennsylvania port
41 Full or half dive
42 Guinness of "The Lavender Hill Mob"
43 Hatfields and McCoys, e.g.
44 Like some goals
45 Radiant glows
46 Commemorative marker
47 Test for size
49 Ricelike pasta
51 Scopes trial org.
52 Respond after reading 'em
54 Grizzly coat
55 Wire service letters

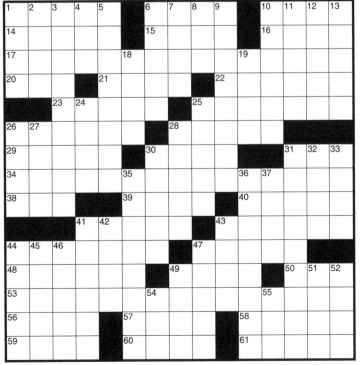

ANSWER, PAGE 93

23

GIRL, INTERRUPTED

ACROSS

1 Blocker of offensive TV material
6 Soccer star Mia
10 Big-eyed birds
14 Destroy by degrees
15 Garfield's canine pal
16 Online activity
17 Communion table symbol
19 Cosmetics name
20 Participating with the team
21 Geoffrey of tales
23 Tiny Tim's instrument
24 "She Loves You" refrain word
26 Jelly flavor
27 Winona of "Girl, Interrupted"
30 Pizzeria order
32 Sought a seat
33 One with a House seat, for short
35 Novelist Tolstoy
36 ___ majesty
37 Whitman poetry book
41 Get smart with
42 Thanksgiving's mo.
43 Distress signal
44 Ala. clock setting
45 Read between the lines
47 Former Winter Palace residents
51 Kick out
53 T, on some tests
55 "Fancy that!"
56 Tough opponents
58 Batter's success
61 Word of mock horror
62 Group with little social status
64 ___-tat
65 Common street name
66 Plus in the ledgers
67 North Sea feeder
68 Withdraws, with "out"
69 Paris subway

DOWN

1 Upholstery fabric
2 Peevish
3 Rapid growth area
4 Prefix meaning "peculiar"
5 "La Bamba" actress Elizabeth
6 Raging masses
7 Tempest in a teapot
8 Monkey business
9 Come together
10 Take place
11 "So?"
12 Note excusing tardiness
13 Plastic component
18 Turn on the waterworks
22 Tree rings indicate it
25 Here, there, and everywhere
28 Hurling stats
29 Gun in the garage
31 Gear teeth
34 Sean of "Mystic River"
36 Girl, and word surrounding this puzzle's theme answers
37 Casino city
38 Rough figure
39 Cajole
40 "Hogwash!"
41 What tourists take in
45 "___ no skin off my nose"
46 Painter Peter Paul
48 All shook up
49 Paul of "Mad About You"
50 Commences
52 Type of chest
54 Musical gift
57 Muppet friend of Rosie
59 Con job
60 Apart from this
63 Clever one

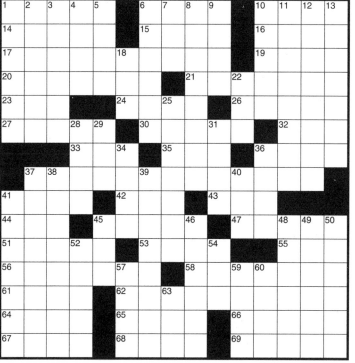

ANSWER, PAGE 94

A DOZEN RABBIT FEET

ACROSS

1 Costa ___
5 Graceful steeds
10 Any miniature golf shot
14 Designed for all grades
15 Palindromic principle
16 "Dancing Queen" quartet
17 Shut rudely, as a door
18 "But only God can ___ tree"
19 Work like a dog
20 Piano adjuster
22 Four-footed Wonderland creature
24 Hosted a roast
26 "Liquor not provided," for short
27 QBs' goals
28 Reno roller
29 "Saturday Night Fever" music
32 Out of fashion
34 Body of soldiers
36 Prevents from leaving
38 Four-footed Easter egg carrier
43 Do over, at a bee
44 Sailor's saint
45 Skeptical grunt
48 Inflict, as havoc
50 Actress Ullmann
51 IOC member
52 Onassis, to Jackie
54 Money back
56 Four-footed nemesis of Elmer Fudd
60 Fancy parties
61 Proof part
62 "Eat crow" or "talk turkey"
64 Big bag
65 Steed stopper
66 Dame preceder, in football and French
67 Suitable for service
68 Very, in Vichy
69 Like Georgia Brown
70 Wasp's home

DOWN

1 Took it easy
2 Throw some light on
3 Take the risk
4 Anouk of "La Dolce Vita"
5 Modern-day money source
6 Reprimand, with "out"
7 "Puppy Love" singer Paul
8 Suds container
9 Mike Hammer portrayer Keach
10 Hiker's route
11 German subs
12 Ford classics
13 Author Gay
21 Dreaded ink color, for students
23 Driver's invitation
25 Some are compact
30 Store display
31 More adorable
33 Cough (up)
35 Maryland athlete, for short
37 Word before system
39 "28 Days" subject
40 Completely isolated
41 Apes
42 Pair chair
45 Part of HHH
46 Loan shark
47 One of Bart's sisters
49 Suds container
53 Archaeological digs
55 Twirler's stick
57 Babies in blue
58 Evening, in ads
59 Olden times
63 NYC opera venue, with "The"

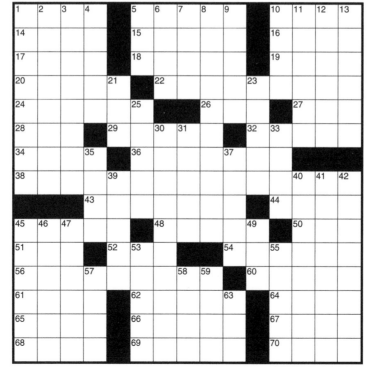

ANSWER, PAGE 79

25

SHAKESPEARE FROM THE REAR

ACROSS

1 Sparkling wine city
5 Bob and Elizabeth, for two
10 Did a take-off on
14 Little piggies
15 Dizzying designs
16 Change addresses
17 Last minute study advice to a friend of Julius Caesar?
19 Breakfast spread
20 On top of, in the world of poetry
21 Birds' partners, in sex ed
22 Read, as a bar code
23 Sang notes without a break
25 With 46-Across, Woolf's rewrite of Othello?
28 Blood category
29 Blood container
30 Ill. clock setting
31 "Amadeus" antagonist
34 Alan or Cheryl
35 Lady Macbeth's cry against spinning toys?
38 Omar of "ER"
39 Takes from the outside
40 Labor Day mo.
41 False god of the Old Testament
42 River to the Rio Grande
46 See 25-Across
48 Bach piece, perhaps
50 Wear at the edges
51 Make a mistake
52 ___ Tin Tin
53 Jagger of rock
54 Shakespeare featured by PBS?
57 On-target
58 Bathsheba's first husband
59 "Why should ___ you?"
60 Ferret physicians
61 Brainy bunch
62 Dijon dad

DOWN

1 Without profit
2 Very much
3 Begin to cry
4 School of thought
5 Heart recipient, e.g.
6 Declined, with "out"
7 Neighbor of Thailand
8 Ending for north or south
9 Hog home
10 Company that merged with BP
11 Icy area to the north or south
12 Seemingly contradictory chance
13 In excelsis ___
18 Out of the country
22 Fifth note on the scale
24 Takes a breather
25 Shown on TV, e.g.
26 Hotel employees
27 Flower shop letters
29 Open to bribery
32 Bochco legal drama
33 Clarification starter
34 Solitary sort
35 Start shooting
36 Blow to the chin, often
37 Start of a basketball game
38 That, south of the border
41 Baby in blue bootees, maybe
43 "It's Too Late" singer/writer King
44 "Platoon" director Stone
45 House that's the counterpart of the House
47 "For goodness ___!"
48 Musical endings
49 Uproar
51 Impish smile
53 Teen tube fave
54 London derrière
55 "___ we having fun yet?"
56 Pup's bite

ANSWER, PAGE 80

WAY TO GOH!

ACROSS

1 Ride in a plane without flying
5 Dynamite ingredient, briefly
10 Bug-eyed
14 In the sack
15 Yellowish earth tone
16 Shown as it happens
17 "The Flintstones" pet
18 Sarcastic gibe
19 Lendl of tennis
20 Gasp done from one's feet?
22 Big swig
23 President before Wilson
24 Tending to business
26 Hummable, perhaps
29 Ocean current
31 Letters before Pinafore
34 Between ports
35 Chocolate source
37 Economize in staging a Japanese dance-drama?
40 "Final Jeopardy" feature
41 It smells
42 Printer's widths
43 Gets on in years
44 Auction participant
46 Phnom ___, Cambodia
48 Teetotaler's order
49 Smooth-talking
51 Homer Simpson's martial arts "Oops!"?
57 Roast beef order
58 Stan's costar
59 Land of shamrocks
60 Arab ruler
61 Artist Max
62 Got a perfect score on
63 Light bulb unit
64 Skeptical
65 Swear by, with "on"

DOWN

1 Young 'uns
2 To some degree
3 Lucy Lawless TV role
4 "Makes no difference"
5 Advise
6 Defeatist's words
7 Tough guy
8 City near Tahoe
9 Generally approved
10 Suspect's story
11 Agree (to)
12 Track shape
13 Courteous chap
21 Dit's partner, in Morse code
25 ___ tide
26 Indian division
27 Les of Clinton's cabinet
28 Dedication, in sports
29 Andrew Marvell's "___ Coy Mistress"
30 Rapper on "Law & Order: SVU"
32 En ___ (as a group)
33 Curl one's lip
35 Tag along
36 Go on and on with someone
38 Oomph
39 Late-show watcher
44 Big Apple street, with "the"
45 Rhoda's TV mom
47 Film critic Roger
48 Vail visitor
49 Became an adult, with "up"
50 Tibetan holy man
52 To the sheltered side
53 North Sea feeder
54 Cut into cubes
55 Pitcher Hershiser
56 Delilah portrayer Lamarr

ANSWER, PAGE 83

27

STAR-CROSSED

ACROSS

1 Czech or Serb, e.g.
5 Idiot box
10 Full of oneself
14 One-third of a war film title
15 Trail follower
16 Round of applause
17 Present-day Persia
18 "___ bad moon rising ..."
19 Peruvian native
20 "Risky Business" star
23 Fifth Avenue retailer
24 High-five, for one
25 Canine star
28 Landlord's contract
31 The bounding main
32 "The Birds" star
36 From scratch
37 Musical comedy star Victor
38 Muddy ground
39 "G.I. Jane" star
41 French capital, in song
42 Island in the Philippines
43 "Key Largo" star Lauren
44 River residue
46 Get dirty
47 "Pursued" star
54 Early political caucus state
55 Blacksmith's block
56 College in New Rochelle
57 Hang decorations on
58 Tommyrot
59 Breakfast dining area
60 Deep desires
61 Milquetoast
62 Fashion mag

DOWN

1 Show signs of life
2 Folk tales and such
3 "Ahab the ___" (Ray Stevens song)
4 "Eraser" star
5 "Growing Pains" star Alan
6 Travelers' documents
7 Timetable, for short
8 Extra-wide shoe spec
9 Coal carrier
10 "Sweet Charity" star
11 Unexpected help
12 Take the lid off of
13 "Morning" in Melbourne
21 Abel's assassin
22 Greek height
25 Put ammo into
26 Teen tribulation
27 Come across as
28 "The Maltese Falcon" star Peter
29 Beat by a whisker
30 Had a bite
32 Underlying cause
33 Old Italian coin
34 Hershiser of baseball
35 The hero usually triumphs in the final one
37 "Whew!"
40 New York nine
41 Beach plaything
43 "Father Dowling Mysteries" star Tom
44 Driftwood site
45 "Rich Man, Poor Man" novelist Shaw
46 Barbershop sounds
47 "The ___ So Nice They Named It Twice" (New York, New York)
48 Skin designs, for short
49 Letters on a cross
50 Rival of Hertz
51 Hammer or sickle
52 Chemical compound
53 Clear, as leaves

ANSWER, PAGE 84

INTIMATE FRONDS

ACROSS

1 Bart Maverick's brother
5 "Exodus" author Leon
9 Moonshine maker
14 Niagara Falls sound
15 Cool off, like a collie
16 Comical Kovacs
17 Actually
19 Hotelier Helmsley
20 Horticultural advice
22 Can't stomach
23 All-night flight
24 Gun barrel cleaner
28 Exhibitors' event
30 Ancient Troy
31 Pottery oven
32 Slight advantage

36 With 50-Across, reason to ignore the advice
39 Spilled the beans
40 ___ many words
41 Comedian/violinist Jack
42 Apt name for a Dalmatian
43 The Rockies and the Andes, e.g.
44 Hand-washer of the Gospels
48 Blueprint
50 See 36-Across
56 Easily-rocked boat
57 Types of "whiskered" swimmers
58 Eventually become

59 Prefix meaning "eight"
60 Thompson of "Sense and Sensibility"
61 Projection room items
62 Crystal ball gazer
63 Lucy's hubby

DOWN

1 Londoner or Liverpudlian, e.g.
2 Columnist Barrett
3 "Fatha" Hines
4 Space odyssey
5 Dispatch, as data
6 "Something to Talk About" vocalist Bonnie
7 Originally
8 Eyelid ailment

9 Merchant
10 Tire pattern
11 Words with hole or all
12 Like a clogged dryer vent
13 Alternative to buy
18 On our field
21 Word processor command
24 Social reformer Jacob
25 Second name in inventions
26 Personal air
27 Ladder crosspiece
29 Part of a.k.a.
31 Casino game
32 Carl Sagan's "The Dragons of ___"
33 Fender nick
34 Barry or Kelly

35 Ben and Jerry's rival
37 Spiteful one
38 River that feeds the Congo
42 Brews, as tea
43 Sought the office of
44 Indiana cager
45 Totally absurd
46 Paul of "Hollywood Squares"
47 In conflict with, with "of"
49 Starbucks selection
51 Sgts. and cpls.
52 Previously owned
53 Woeful words
54 Valuable stones
55 Lou's "La Bamba" costar

ANSWER, PAGE 87

HI! DEFINITION

ACROSS

1 Light classical orchestra
5 Vacuum tube filler
10 Sticking point
14 White and black snack
15 Part of AWOL
16 Top of the line
17 Protection from ultraviolet rays
19 Managers' degs.
20 "Hi!"
22 Talk back to
23 Ionian isle
26 Forgoes food
29 Curly coif
32 Part of a royal flush
33 Tennis great Arthur
34 "Hi!"
37 Hammer-wielding deity
38 Inventor Howe
39 A, as in Edison?
40 "Hi!"
42 Some Wharton grads
43 Miner's matter
44 Cheat, in slang
45 Hot-tempered
46 Blend with traffic
48 On the calm side
50 "Hi!"
57 Country music's Dixie Chicks, e.g.
59 Strip in a locker room?
60 Dog of "Dennis the Menace"
61 Go ballistic, with "out"
62 Gillette product
63 ABA member
64 Thin-skinned
65 Poet Silverstein

DOWN

1 Game on felt
2 Soup pasta
3 Lowly laborer
4 Writers of "Yesterday" and "Tomorrow," e.g.
5 "___ well"
6 Lots of paper
7 Marvin of Motown
8 Kind of mitt
9 Roman fiddler
10 Small role
11 Opponent of Ulysses S. Grant
12 Actress Alicia
13 "Scream" director Craven
18 LAX postings
21 Dundee dweller
24 Passion
25 On pins and needles
26 Understand
27 Off the ship
28 Set of his-and-her towels, perhaps
29 Linda Lavin sitcom
30 Strong criticism
31 "Lady Sings the Blues" star Diana
34 Big sandwich
35 Some Ivy Leaguers
36 Extensive estates
41 Huxtable son
45 Bit of greenery
47 Disney dog
48 Ready to hit
49 Like a trireme in trouble
51 Off one's rocker
52 Land measure
53 Professional charges
54 Swear word
55 Folklore fiend
56 Patricia of "Hud"
57 Singer's syllable
58 Wagon track

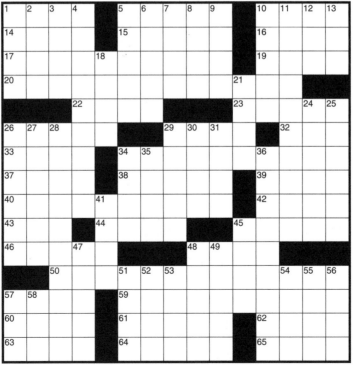

ANSWER, PAGE 88

TRANSIT BENEATH

ACROSS

1 Some S&L offerings
4 State in a nutshell
9 Brief brawl
14 Ad follower?
15 Brunch serving
16 Was sore
17 Folk singer DiFranco
18 With 24-Across, abolitionist network
20 Derive by reasoning
22 Put one's name on
23 GPs, e.g.
24 See 18-Across
26 Pyramid, to a Pharaoh
28 "I thought this might be of interest"
29 Fruit, or nutty as a fruitcake
32 Palindromic cry
35 In the wee hours
38 "I knew ___ along!"
39 Part of a sandwich chain
43 Spiritual
44 "Swan Lake" skirt
45 Down in the dumps
46 Sound reproduction systems
48 Army cops: Abbr.
51 Its teeth point in all directions
52 Strapless garments
57 Out ___ limb
59 Signs over
61 Bochco TV drama
62 Urbane urban male
65 Be behind
66 Out in front
67 One way to live
68 Public image, briefly
69 Potato chip feature, perhaps
70 Up to now
71 Banned pesticide

DOWN

1 Preside over
2 Summer or Reed
3 Trekkies' field
4 Rush
5 Coffee container
6 TV, radio, etc.
7 Flip
8 Executive extra
9 Cynical
10 "The Name of the Rose" author Umberto
11 Digital detail?
12 Watch over
13 Track numbers
19 "___ life!"
21 Little toymaker of lore
25 Like many a garage floor
27 Calculating course
29 Ready to hit the hay
30 To boot
31 Whole lot
32 Clearance condition
33 Chase game
34 Gave up
36 P.M.'s
37 Capote, to friends
40 "___ off to see the Wizard"
41 Part of a phone number
42 Ready for the dentist's drill
47 Bauxite and others
49 Air rifle projectile
50 B&O stop
52 Home of "all my ex's," in a song
53 Shylock's business
54 Supplication start, maybe
55 "Knocked" on the door, like Lassie
56 Won every game from
57 Bridge expert Sharif
58 Radar's favorite pop
60 Crème-crème filling
63 Old T-shirt, perhaps
64 Grow older

ANSWER, PAGE 91

SIZE MATTERS

ACROSS

1 Pop singer Tori
5 Prepare to shoot
10 Barn birds
14 Fountain treat or brewer's grain
15 In other words
16 Biweekly tide
17 Prefix with European
18 Part of a step
19 Rooney of "60 Minutes"
20 Big head
23 What voters use to choose
24 South Sea souvenirs
26 WWII zone
27 They tend church regularly
31 Trial and tribulation
32 Sleuth Wolfe
34 Prefix with type
35 Wash
36 Teetotalers
37 Trims back
38 Encouraging words
39 Big Foot
42 Explorer Sebastian
45 Face-to-face exams
49 Parseghian of football
50 Body on Uzbekistan's border
56 Like a good golf score
57 Big hand
60 Grease monkey's job
61 Gift recipient
62 "Peter Pan" pirate
63 Scandinavian metropolis
64 Cara of "Fame"
65 Barbershop sound
66 Archie or Jughead
67 Cozy places
68 Dolts, in Dover

DOWN

1 "Is that true about yours truly?"
2 Dangerous carnivore
3 The Stars and Stripes
4 Seat for a suds sipper
5 Dangerous buildings
6 Valhalla VIP
7 "___ la vie!"
8 Internet surfer
9 Most authoritarian
10 Studio sign
11 Left
12 Favorite female
13 Cloak-and-dagger type
21 Avoid responsibility, with "out"
22 Funnyman Bill, familiarly
23 Give in
25 Goes out with
28 Baghdad's country
29 Hose hue
30 Big Apple ballpark, once
33 ___ buco
35 Oz coward portrayer Bert
40 To some extent
41 Frosty's "eyes"
42 Where to find wheels
43 Build a fire under
44 Showy ornament
46 Homecoming guests
47 Freak out
48 Big week in TV
51 "The Thinker" sculptor
52 Prefix with mentioned
53 Bowling alley divisions
54 All tuckered out
55 Blades with guarded tips
58 Light filler
59 Pt. of NCAA

ANSWER, PAGE 92

DATA BANCROFT

ACROSS

1 Refs' decisions
6 Napoleon's exile isle
10 Joel's "Cabaret" costar
14 Alaskan islander
15 Like proverbial unobtainable grapes
16 Woolf's "A Room of ___ Own"
17 Org. for racial equality
18 Landed
19 Gone to Davy Jones's locker
20 Bancroft's role in "The Miracle Worker"
23 Wasn't up-front with
24 "In the room the women come and go / Talking of Michelangelo" writer
27 Outdated Asian map abbr.
28 Lanchester of cinema
31 Ad with a freebie
32 Rodeo bull
34 Pie à la ___
35 Bancroft's role in "The Graduate"
38 Patella site
40 Changes the decor of
41 Test answers in blue books
44 Miles per hour, e.g.
45 MDs who unload the stork, so to speak
48 Rings of rubber
50 Money set aside
52 Bancroft's role in "Jesus of Nazareth"
55 Gunfight challenge
57 Y chromosome carrier
58 Passed (time), with "away"
59 "Rubyfruit Jungle" novelist ___ Mae Brown
60 Pitching wedge, for example
61 Come next
62 Bishop of the Rat Pack
63 Jazz singer James
64 Vast extents

DOWN

1 Many "streets" of Venice
2 "Jagged Little Pill" singer Morissette
3 It scores one in horseshoes
4 Perfectly clear
5 Where Benedict XVI was first seen in public
6 Isaac's slightly older son
7 Veg out
8 Well-muscled
9 Van Gogh or Picasso
10 Atomic research center site
11 Of one accord
12 Kind of Buddhism
13 Put the question to
21 From the nearest star
22 Formation of flying geese
25 Ref. room offering
26 Three, in Napoli
29 New York restaurateur Toots
30 "Waves of grain" color
32 Secede from the Union, e.g.
33 Elton John Broadway musical
35 Salt who passes the salt, e.g.
36 Picked up on
37 Enjoyed a plank on a playground
38 Gunpowder holder
39 Code-breaking govt. group
42 "So's ___ old man!"
43 Get in the way of
45 Ultimatum's end
46 Get ready for a test
47 Bergman and Garbo
49 Like Mensa members
51 "Crazy" singer Patsy
53 Very much
54 Rowlands of "The Notebook"
55 Erving, to fans
56 Brazilian vacation spot

ANSWER, PAGE 95

BACK AND FORTH

ACROSS

1 Cool rapper?
5 Is in the hole
9 Easy ___
14 Matador's foe, or brand for those who mow
15 "Gilmore Girls" daughter
16 Job for a daredevil
17 Metal for recycling
19 Patronize, as a restaurant
20 Blue funk?
22 Speedway competition
23 Cornstalk offshoot
24 Corkscrew-tailed animal
25 First European to see the Mississippi
27 Witty Wilde
29 Vanilla cookies often found in banana pudding
31 Red Skelton's ___ Kadiddlehopper
34 Mideast chief
36 Construction site hoist
37 Where the heart is, they say
38 Cut off
40 On the ocean
41 Computer screen pictures
43 Overstuff
44 Six years, for a senator
45 Provincial speech
47 Truth stretchers
49 Picked up
51 CBS forensic drama, for short
52 "Just ___ suspected!"
55 Bus. major's study
56 Like a cheesy dish?
59 Freeway divisions
61 State of Lake Wobegon
62 Andes beast of burden
63 "___ homo!"
64 Ever so proper
65 Give permission for
66 Tea leaves reader
67 Change for a five

DOWN

1 Knocker's reply
2 Hot chocolate drink
3 Dropped fly, for example
4 Sticky-tongued fly-catcher
5 Ear, nose, and throat
6 Scrabble and such
7 Ending for switch
8 Ecclesiastical gathering
9 Wall St. group
10 Topnotch stoolie?
11 Helped to relax
12 With no way out
13 Luncheon add-on
18 Emulates the weasel
21 Kitten call
26 Pouch in the body
27 Fish sign?
28 Paris, to Romeo
30 Clothing joint
31 Bit of chocolate
32 It doesn't need the area code
33 Showing strong feelings
35 Tendency to be reserved
39 Former newscaster Harry
42 Pose for a pic
46 Where a rev.-to-be may study Revelation
48 Teeming (with)
50 Maggie Smith and Judi Dench
52 Deck out
53 Composer Erik
54 Mosque officials
55 Raines of filmdom
57 Vegas rollers
58 Classic Bruin nickname
60 Tool with teeth

ANSWER, PAGE 96

34

PEN PALS

ACROSS

1 Theory of the beginning
8 Lay away
15 Wake-up call
16 Never, perhaps
17 HOG
19 Black and white piano parts
20 Hide a mike on
21 Mineo of movies
22 Suffix for verb
25 Former New York mayor Abe
28 PIG
35 The screaming-meemies
36 Flip out
37 Billboard messages
38 Superman's nemesis Luthor
39 Catchword from "The Simpsons"
41 In the distance
42 "___ my case"
44 Conscious
46 SWINE
49 Word before donna or ballerina
50 Canonized Mlle.
51 Enthusiast, in slang
54 Salon offering
56 In the distance
60 RAZORBACK
65 Toy racer
66 Card-carrying civil servant?
67 Says it's so
68 Insectivorous insect

DOWN

1 Pitcher's flub
2 "Dies ___"
3 Like slasher films
4 Hits the road
5 Chemical suffix
6 "Miss Saigon" setting, breifly
7 Healthy look
8 Naps noisily
9 Attacked violently
10 Needing no Dr.'s prescription
11 Rogers or Clark
12 SASEs, e.g.
13 Pac-10 team
14 Avenger Emma
18 Leg bone
23 More gracefully slender
24 Belfast's country
26 Possibly will decline to
27 Earth-friendly prefix
28 Committee head
29 Prefix with electric
30 Thing of value
31 Give the thumbs-down to
32 More merry
33 Barely winning
34 Streisand title role
39 To God, to Nero
40 Treaters' offer
43 Fuel additive
44 Healing signs
45 In the best of all possible worlds
47 Tries to bite
48 Slings mud at
51 Far-out travel agency?
52 WWW addresses
53 Some wins for pugilists in shorts, for short
55 Crib cry
57 Disaster relief org.
58 ___ impasse
59 Monthly payment for many
61 Absorbed, as the cost
62 Business machine co.
63 Adhesive for feathers
64 Finger-pointer's cry

ANSWER, PAGE 81

35

POOL PARTY

ACROSS

1 Sales people
5 Pueblo material
10 What you can take from me
14 Acted like
15 Show to be false
16 Request for permission
17 Flamingo or stork, e.g.
19 Like a yellow banana
20 Lemon
21 Becomes free of
22 Free-for-all
23 Hint at, with "to"
25 Doctor's org.
27 Wray of "King Kong"
28 New drivers, often
29 Cajun side
32 Schick competitor
33 Dry, in a wine cellar
34 Gradually withdrawn
35 "The Singing Cowboy"
38 Magician's hiding place, stereotypically
41 British WWII fliers
42 Picket fence features
46 Source of lemons, sometimes
48 Welcome sound, to one's ears
49 Hadrian's "hello"
50 Cereal box letters
51 Bright yellow
52 Fork over
54 Succeed in life
57 Lab animal
58 Guitarist Clapton
59 Constant talker
61 Golden rule preposition
62 Crawled out of bed
63 Make tracks
64 Hammerhead part
65 Sleep sound
66 "The Untouchables," e.g.

DOWN

1 Unanalyzed information
2 Shoulder piece
3 Street vendor
4 Star Wars initials
5 Have words
6 Young socialites
7 Memorial notice
8 Tuition check taker
9 LAX posting
10 Real estate unit
11 Rear end feature
12 How to go from church
13 Under the table
18 Dozes off
22 Part of MGM
24 Like new wine
26 Calendar letter sequence
29 Wallace of "E.T."
30 Words of empathy
31 Heater of the future
33 Links legend Sam
36 Frequent foe of Navratilova
37 Former Arab confed.
38 Manage to find
39 Shirley's roomie
40 Solitary one
43 In the main
44 Stolen at sea
45 Grim Reaper accessories
47 "Creature From the Black ___"
48 Old-time schoolteacher
51 Seize, in a saying
53 Desktop symbol
55 "Beetle Bailey" dog
56 Fab number, in rock-'n'-roll
59 Classic two-seaters
60 "Scram!"

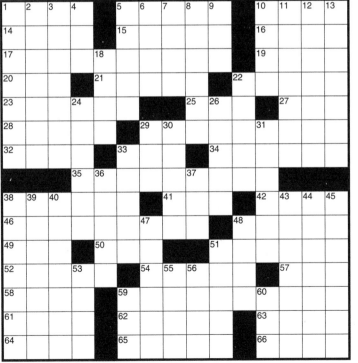

ANSWER, PAGE 82

ENOUGH!

ACROSS

1 Fishnet, for example
5 Nightclub employee
10 Earth's dominant society, in a Wahlberg film
14 Peace Nobelist Wiesel
15 Onetime daytime host O'Donnell
16 Teen party
17 Sheridan and Sothern
18 Take as one's own
19 Tennis pro Nastase
20 Makes holes while wearing dressy shoes?
23 Neighbor of Minn.
24 Denver summer hrs.
25 Sportsperson, of course?
26 Stiff, or like a staff
28 On the peak of
30 Sailor's yes
31 Free from care
33 Served superbly
34 Make a sketch of guards and tackles?
37 Opposed to, in Dogpatch
39 Say
40 Roth plan
41 Stretch across
43 Drives dangerously
47 Hair salon item
49 Hosp. units
50 Poem full of praise
51 Make fun of a body part?
55 Second word in most fairy tales
56 SeaWorld star
57 Häagen-Dazs alternative
58 Outfielder's cry
59 Hourglass, e.g.
60 Corn bread loaf
61 Jury member
62 In broad daylight
63 Polliwog's place

DOWN

1 Where goats gobble grass
2 Weather whipping boy
3 Serenade
4 Big name in oil
5 Hot off the press
6 Beckett's no-show
7 Has the stage
8 Good to taste, or bad to smell
9 "C'mon!"
10 Disney mermaid
11 Oater Caucasian
12 Allegedly harmful look
13 Hits the roof
21 "... ___ man with seven wives"
22 Move like a bunny
27 Fix sox
28 Visibly frightened
29 Swarm (with)
32 Name on a razor
33 "My Way" writer Paul
34 Receiver sound
35 Place for a case
36 Start of a legal conclusion
37 Cause of inflation?
38 Devoted fan of a band
41 Washington VIP
42 Magician's cry
44 ___ doll
45 Radio comedian dubbed "The Perfect Fool"
46 Had a hunch
48 Not the glad-handing sort
49 Future star
52 Hood's blade
53 Fortune's partner
54 Johnny of "Pirates of the Caribbean"

ANSWER, PAGE 85

MARCHING ORDERS

ACROSS

1 Desi Arnaz, by birth
6 Per unit
10 Time, going forward or backward
14 Athenian assembly area
15 RC, e.g.
16 One of the deadly sins
17 Part of RSVP
18 Pre-Soviet sovereign
19 Nest noise
20 Fast food chain
22 Within reach
24 Grazing spot
25 Little green men, or green card holders
26 Double
31 Windy City airport
32 Greek liqueur
33 Ref's call, in boxing
36 Ore deposit
37 Mail carrier's beat
39 Go after
40 Commandment pronoun
41 Front-page stuff
42 Pasta shape
43 Cole's string section
47 Big exams
48 Modus operandi
49 Nastassja of "Terminal Velocity"
50 Words before a walk
55 Gymnast Korbut
56 Happy face
58 "Pygmalion" flower seller
59 Serious sign
60 Thundering group
61 Museum piece
62 Funeral pile
63 "I did it!"
64 Full of back talk

DOWN

1 Daisy Mae's creator Al
2 Wrinkled fruit
3 Ruth's husband
4 D'backs' home
5 Portman of "Where the Heart Is"
6 Honest-to-goodness
7 Newsgroup message
8 Ending with pay
9 Render powerless
10 Yankee Doodle Dandy, to Uncle Sam?
11 Whom the Bible says to love
12 Bakery fixtures
13 Big Apple enforcement org.
21 With it
23 Brother of Jermaine
25 Border on
26 Lose feathers
27 "Houston, we have a problem"
28 Small sponge cake
29 Number after due
30 Brooklynese pronoun
34 Mustard family vegetable
35 Eye amorously
37 Stop signal
38 Night fliers
39 "Pipe down!"
41 Neighbor of Minn.
42 Salon employees
44 Bonkers
45 Kigali's country
46 My gal, in a song
47 Thin and light
49 Former Surgeon General
50 Shuttlecock
51 Dog biter
52 Masseuse's supplies
53 Israeli submachine guns
54 Risqué
57 Stephen of "Breakfast on Pluto"

ANSWER, PAGE 86

SPECIFIC CONGRATS ...

ACROSS

1 Nobel Institute city
5 Climbers' obstacles
10 Genesis kingdom
14 Non-numerical phone button
15 Nostalgic fashion trend
16 Follow the directions of
17 Bear among the stars
18 On a leash
19 Breaks off
20 ... for Bush?
23 Features of baseball caps
24 Explorer Vasco ___
26 Prelude, for short
27 Pts. for the Packers
30 "Not to worry!"
31 Austrian article
32 Practice exercises
35 Suffix with serpent
36 Sea near the Caspian
38 First of Caesar's claims
39 They're neither Dem. nor Rep.
40 ... for a Hail Mary catcher?
43 "Indeed," in the Bible
44 Second name in sci-fi
45 Family vehicle
48 Put down, in slang
51 Word in an Oscar acceptance speech
55 Poker declaration
56 Copper coins
58 Moisturizer ingredient
59 ... for guards?
62 Fancy-schmancy
63 Simulated battle
64 Women's shoes
65 Took the wheel

DOWN

1 Buckeyes' sch.
2 Noodle holder, at times
3 Camel's backbreaker, proverbially
4 Soapbox topper
5 New parents' purchases
6 Janet of the Clinton cabinet
7 6-Down, for one: Abbr.
8 Pirate potable
9 Did a farm job
10 Come into one's own
11 Dumbbell, or bell sound
12 When asked for
13 OR workers
21 Baseball nickname
22 Rowers pull them
23 Ricky Martin's "Livin' La ___ Loca"
25 Fires abruptly
27 Big name in model trains
28 Compete in cars
29 Battle of behemoths
33 Musical meter maid
34 Carter of sitcoms
37 Succeed in a coop, or fail in most else
39 Running things
41 Longing
42 No longer an option
45 Muscular strength
46 DeBeque in "South Pacific"
47 Cut into cubes
48 Charger's woes
49 Powers that be
50 Crockpot concoctions
52 "Are you calling me ___?"
53 Shirker's phrase
54 On edge, with "up"
56 Heavenly Hash holder
57 Fitzgerald forte
60 ___ alai
61 Script ending?

ANSWER, PAGE 89

VOCATIONS FOR DUMMIES

ACROSS

1 Entertainers with no dialogue
6 Barrelhead bills
10 "Let's get crackin'!"
14 As a whole
15 Ready for plucking
16 Juno, to the Greeks
17 One who hits a tackling dummy
19 Cutlass maker, briefly
20 "My goodness!"
21 Frozen fruit treat
23 Rams' better halves
25 Notorious cow owner
26 One who speaks for a dummy
31 "My goodness!"
32 Circuit protector
33 Halloween mo.
36 Caps on the Clyde
37 Cosmetics maker Lauder
39 Limp watch painter
40 Smallest bill
41 Cracker topper
42 WWII riveter
43 One who breathes into a dummy
47 Slanted to the right
49 Matt Damon to Greg Kinnear, in "Stuck on You"
50 Citizen soldiers' group
52 Rio beach in a 1964 hit song
57 Fully qualified
58 One who pins material on a dummy
60 Will of "The Waltons"
61 Top 10, e.g.
62 Plain as day
63 Slips up
64 Bothers, with "at"
65 "One Flew Over the Cuckoo's Nest" author

DOWN

1 Ho Chi ___
2 The skinny
3 Teen's hangout
4 Jed's daughter
5 Onion ring preparers, e.g.
6 Embroidery yarn
7 Sharpshooter's gift
8 Sauna bath sites
9 Unwise guard duty assignment for a fox
10 Tedious tasks
11 Crunchy bread named for an Australian opera singer
12 Cry from the bench
13 Like inclement weather
18 Bedtime prayer start
22 "Night" author Wiesel
24 Most out of shape
26 West Wing threat
27 Richard of "Love Me Tender"
28 Verbal abuser
29 Sixes for the 49ers: Abbr.
30 Doris Day song title starter
34 Advertising award
35 Level at a playing field
37 "Life of Brian" star
38 Ugly as ___
39 Dwarf with glasses
41 Daphne of "Frasier," for one
42 Go ape
44 Wire-bending tool
45 Dances like Chubby Checker
46 Splits open
47 Public persona
48 River of Rome
51 Diva's delight
53 Pew area
54 Barely makes, with "out"
55 Little more than
56 Culturally pretentious
59 Superlative suffix

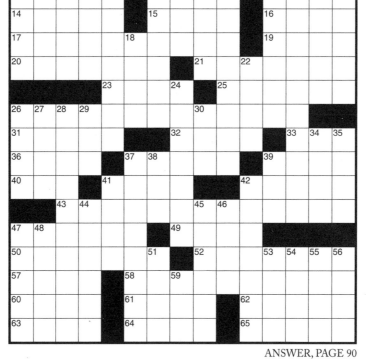

ANSWER, PAGE 90

SWITCH POSITIONS

ACROSS

1 Skip over
5 Compact data holders
10 Yank ally
14 Tease mercilessly
15 "Dallas" matriarch
16 Continental money
17 "The Thin Man" pooch
18 Be a good student
19 Green-eyed monster
20 Rave review for sexual abstinence?
23 Saloon serving
24 The Orange of college sports
27 Beatles' manager Brian
30 ___ Island Ferry
31 Online commerce
34 Empire State Building climber
35 Insult continuously?
40 Bunkum
41 Bar where sailors may stop
42 Country singer Ronnie
45 Slogs through
50 Slab of ground beef
53 Wellspring
54 Christmas bureau?
57 Lysol target
59 Dressed like a judge
60 Go with the ___
61 Parents' choice
62 On the wide side
63 French 101 verb
64 Herring type
65 Contract conditions
66 Like Easter eggs

DOWN

1 Delphic medium
2 Accident
3 Badges with names
4 Sugar bowl, creamer, etc.
5 Supermarket section
6 "Can ___ you in on a little secret?"
7 Does in
8 Garry Moore sidekick Durward
9 Men of La Mancha
10 Male eye candy
11 Desert
12 Sportscaster Cross
13 Cracker Jack surprise
21 Like a trapped kitty, perhaps
22 Unlikely, as a chance
25 Fax or FedEx
26 Part of the U.K.
28 Ending with Juan
29 Votes against
32 Kabibble of Kay Kyser's band
33 Plunderer's take
35 Pâté de ___ gras
36 "Where the wind comes sweeping down the plain"
37 Returned to mint condition
38 Way off
39 Something of little substance
40 "I'm thinking ..."
43 Musketeer motto word
44 "Murder on the Orient Express" detective
46 Tipped, as a hat
47 At fault
48 Cry for more
49 Like some prunes
51 Reader computer program company
52 Big name in pencils
55 Positive response to Aunt Polly
56 Poems of praise
57 Positions switched in this puzzle
58 "Camptown Races" syllable

ANSWER, PAGE 93

GO WASH OUT YOUR MOUTH!

ACROSS
1 Margarine slices
5 Prickly plants
10 Singer Amos
14 Leave out
15 "Get along now!"
16 Baking place
17 They can "listen" without hearing
19 Rowlands of filmdom
20 Primes the poker pot
21 Bad language
23 Pullet places
25 Castle in a board game
26 Small peg
27 Bristle at
29 Pooh-pooh
31 Gad about
35 Change alternative, in some vending machines
36 Whip mark

39 Chemical reaction, for short
40 Nothing but
41 Unwelcome obligation
42 Diner sign
44 Tattered and torn
46 Continent separators
49 Utmost degree
50 Whitney and Wallach
54 Rock layers
56 With 61-Across, why 17-Across can clean up 21-Across
59 Dozen for a sweetheart
60 Day saver
61 See 56-Across
63 Noncommittal words

64 Nick of "Hotel Rwanda"
65 Partner of rank and serial number
66 Prefix with second
67 Dozen for a recovery group
68 Check for fingerprints

DOWN
1 Like some opposites
2 Key of all white notes
3 Move through the tulips, in song
4 Treadmill ordeal
5 T.J. "Stonewall" Jackson's country
6 O.K. in any outlet

7 Heart of France
8 Trunk of the body
9 Linda Ronstadt's "___ Easy"
10 Fast-food option
11 Extra meaning
12 One who gives Caesar what is Caesar's, e.g.
13 Sort of
18 Fragrant compound
22 Parts of a mo.
24 Drum kit component
28 "___ yellow ribbon ..."
30 Be won over to a new position
32 Summer hrs. in California
33 Art gallery district

34 Biz bigwigs
36 Gotten tedious
37 Something detested
38 Follower of a German Protestant
43 Backward-looking
45 Archery bow wood
47 Bahamas port
48 Prepares, as milk for cappuccino
51 Yards of grass
52 "Some Like ___"
53 Actor's minimum wage
55 So far
57 Toy on a string
58 URL starter
62 "By all means!"

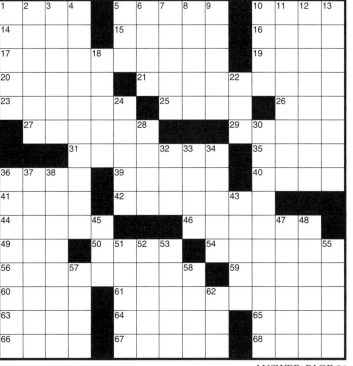

ANSWER, PAGE 94

STICK TO CARROT STICKS

ACROSS

1 Publisher Adolph
5 Wing it
10 Take a deep breath
14 Nursery supply
15 O. Henry literary device
16 Razor handle?
17 Submarine order
18 Interior design
19 Working stiff
20 Start of a request on a sign at the zoo
23 Cheap hairpiece
24 Like bell-bottoms
25 Legislation leading to a Boston Harbor raid
27 Prefix with meter
28 Gillespie's genre
31 Middle of the request
32 "Jesus Christ Superstar" soloist
34 Seemingly forever
35 They eat no meat
38 No Emily Post expert
40 Big cheese
41 End of the request
44 Lab subj.
45 D.C. fund-raiser
48 Witch's deity
49 Small hill
51 "Wheel of Fortune" buy
52 Addition to the request by 35-Across
57 Throngs
59 "Don't even bother"
60 Nigerian-born singer
61 At the apex of
62 Acquired relative
63 Timeline segments
64 Appealing
65 Pastrami places
66 Ocular woe

DOWN

1 No newbie
2 Like a snake that's all wound up
3 "Can't get out of it"
4 Campaign tactic
5 Man or gal Friday
6 Scott of a noted court decision
7 Off your rocker
8 Privy to
9 How some learn
10 Easy mark
11 Goes over again
12 Brother of Harpo
13 Do a surfboard stunt
21 Edna Ferber novel
22 Golf supporter
26 "A Bell for ___"
29 Roar in a ring
30 Ways of righteousness, in Psalm 23
31 Flowerless plants
32 Prefix on names of durable products
33 Eastern ideal
35 You use it to talk
36 Trade watchdog
37 "Take ___!"
38 Nassau's country
39 Like monotonous Johnny
42 ABA member
43 Soviet leader Brezhnev
45 Genre of Peter Max
46 24, in 24/7
47 "A Fish Called Wanda" star John
50 They smell
53 Manner of speaking
54 Bottom of a boat
55 Morales of movies
56 Where the church softball team gets benched?
58 Get a load of

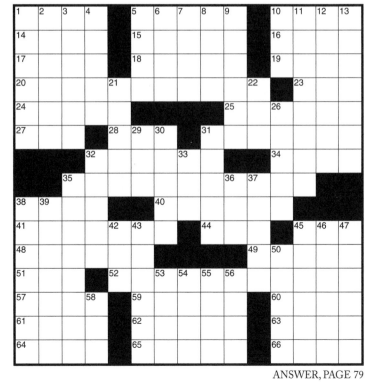

ANSWER, PAGE 79

43

CYBER-CHUCKLE

ACROSS

1 "You don't know the ___ of it!"
5 Mountaintop
9 Comic Poundstone
14 Romanian writer Wiesel
15 Toll unit, sometimes
16 Choir supporter
17 "Don't look ___!"
18 Run the show
19 "Er ... um ..."
20 Cone source
23 Dalmatian detail
24 Gives voice to
27 Almost boils
30 Mom-and-pop org.
31 Ambient musician Brian
33 Lofty standards
34 With 39-Across, boat in a Shirley Temple song
36 Pickling herb
37 Geometry suffix
38 Lie low
39 See 34-Across
42 Designer Ralph
44 Eisenhower's WWII command
45 Born, in the society pages
46 Interviewer Barbara
47 Uses indelicate language
49 Encourage in a way that should be discouraged
50 They interpret literary texts
55 Borden bovine
58 Baltic Sea feeder
59 Tickled-pink feeling
60 Puccini opera
61 Brandy sniffer
62 Do a pitcher's job
63 Manila envelope feature
64 Diploma receiver, briefly
65 Letters for nine-to-fivers

DOWN

1 Do a doctor's job
2 Sax type
3 Elm extension
4 Suffer low self-esteem
5 Ice cream places, e.g.
6 Jumps for joy
7 Friendly nation
8 Stay informed about
9 Pitch on paper
10 Woman's name meaning "loved"
11 Wear and tear
12 Herd's hangout
13 Prince Valiant's son
21 Autobahn auto
22 "What's ___ you?"
25 Bring back on staff
26 Baseball Hall of Famer Duke
27 Move like a crab
28 Numskulls
29 Become less stressed, with "out"
32 Big tournaments
34 Republicans, for short
35 Firmly closed
37 Tries for a Hail Mary
40 Piled up
41 Gilpin of "Frasier"
42 Worked like a dog
43 "Shake ___!" ("Move it!")
46 Poland's Lech
48 "Cast of thousands" films
51 Evidence of forgotten Secret
52 Counterfeit coin
53 Actress Polo of "Beyond Borders"
54 Part of SASE
55 The latest thing in lists: Abbr.
56 Cyber-chuckle hidden in this puzzle's theme entries
57 Fed. benefit source

ANSWER, PAGE 80

HUNGER FOR KNOWLEDGE

ACROSS

1 Sidewalk eatery
5 Uncontrollable masses
9 Tara family name
14 Russia's ___ Mountains
15 Hand cream ingredient
16 Type of button
17 Wall of earth
18 In style and then some
20 Start of a quip
22 Produce in a hurry, with "out"
23 Prepared, an old postage stamp
27 More of the quip
32 Something to believe in
33 Tiniest amount of rice
34 Door frame upright
38 Words before Aquarius
40 Emerald isle
41 T.S. who wrote "April is the cruellest month"
43 Perrier competitor
45 More of the quip
50 More in need of a chill pill
51 Loggers' competition
53 End of the quip
58 Alternative to buying on credit
61 Ancient Briton
62 That's what happens
63 Rowing team, e.g.
64 A really big shoe
65 Mamas' mates
66 Painter Paul
67 Canadian oil company

DOWN

1 Like bits of bouillon
2 "Queen of Soul" Franklin
3 Way off, or offbeat
4 Novelist Leonard
5 Sir's counterpart
6 It's a crock
7 Lightning flash
8 Brother of Abel and Cain
9 Word that may follow eye or grand
10 Dyed-in-the-wool
11 Info collection
12 Fix, as a horse race
13 Crack fighter pilot
19 Circle of angels
21 Heal, like a broken arm
24 "The Bridge on the River ___"
25 Bahrain biggie
26 Unit of force
28 Chinese restaurant drink
29 Fastidious roommate Felix
30 A little thing that irritates a lot
31 Stiff-upper-lip type
34 Rock musician Joan
35 On the less windy side
36 Comportment
37 Neighbor of Namibia
39 Toy seller ___ Schwarz
42 Singers of "I'm a Believer"?
44 Cop in a drug bust
46 Like a bohemian wannabe
47 Glare reducer for the bald?
48 "Dallas" matriarch and namesakes
49 Twos in a deck
52 Bone prefix
54 Deposit with a pawnbroker
55 Ringlet of hair
56 Screenwriter James
57 Rob of "Salem's Lot"
58 Word before talk or rally
59 Gardner of "On the Beach"
60 "Sure thing"

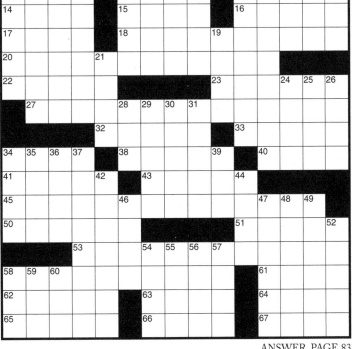

ANSWER, PAGE 83

THE BODY POLITIC

ACROSS

1 Foot curve
5 Former Virginia senator Charles
9 Litmus reddeners
14 Spelling of TV
15 Message beginning
16 Lisa of "The Cosby Show"
17 Representative position
19 Reggae musician, perhaps
20 Summer in the city of Paris
21 Potted plant place
22 One-___ (short play)
23 On the water
25 Warm greeting for voters
27 Antique desk feature
29 Taken care of
30 Make a swap
31 Marker tip material
34 Tobacco pipe tube
35 Where you might shoot pool
38 Democratic donkey designer Thomas
42 Furtive "Hey, you!"
43 MacDowell of "Groundhog Day"
48 Cover completely
50 Flying alone, e.g.
52 Campaign fund
55 Like traditional Disney films
56 Feed, as a fire
57 Bald tire's lack
59 1–1 score, for one
60 Green stuff
61 Political leader
63 "Ragged Dick" author Horatio
64 BBs and bullets
65 Cube designer Rubik
66 Things lacking
67 Bygone leader
68 Pt. of NAACP

DOWN

1 Deep down
2 Support with cheers
3 De Vil of "101 Dalmatians"
4 Hubby's towel word
5 Meet, as expectations
6 Lacking depth and h.
7 Fort in North Carolina
8 ___ nut
9 Rub the wrong way?
10 Bear Bryant and Mike Krzyzewski
11 Quick coffee
12 Thaw in the Cold War
13 Celeb status
18 Click beetle
24 Like the gray mare of song
26 Regarding
28 One-stripers, for short
32 Sounds of hesitation
33 Places where they yell "Cut!"
36 Dueling weapon
37 Chronic ailment
38 Peter Jennings, e.g.
39 Novelist France
40 Repentant miser
41 Went to work on
44 "Fooled you!"
45 They cut calories
46 Delhi dwellers
47 Incited to action
49 Removes with clippers
51 One with a silver tongue
53 Ireland's patron, for short
54 Streetcars
58 Bombeck of "At Wit's End"
62 "Isn't ___ bit like you and me?" (Beatles lyric)

ANSWER, PAGE 84

MORE OR LES

ACROSS

1 Talk with one's hands
5 Huxtable mom
10 Charlie Brown exclamation
14 Grimm character
15 "___ he grown!"
16 K through 12
17 Unwanted stickers?
20 Took pleasure in, with "up"
21 State Farm rival
22 Roman Empire invaders
23 Kevin Costner golf movie
25 Chop suey additive
27 "Bali ___"
28 What a rampager goes on
29 Looks through the keyhole
31 Day before
32 Touch up, at the salon
34 Bonanza finds
35 Italian town without siestas?
38 Hodgepodge
39 Stiffly formal
40 Small batteries
41 Mudville slugger
42 "Just Shoot Me" actor George
46 ___-Magnon
47 "Diamonds ___ Forever"
48 Stand for
49 Daisy Mae's husband
51 In pieces
54 Comic strip prince's son
55 Fab Four with poor timing?
58 Monopoly payment
59 Aussie "bear"
60 Carpenter's clamp
61 Art Deco illustrator
62 "Door's open"
63 Becomes Jell-O

DOWN

1 Beethoven specialty
2 "So that's what you're up to!"
3 Lorne of "Bonanza"
4 Beatty of "Network"
5 Word from a bird to Scrooge?
6 Make it to the end
7 Co. or org.
8 Lacking substance
9 U.S. mail carrier's beat
10 Decorate anew
11 Playing with a full deck
12 Privileged people
13 Pantywaists
18 Victory emblem
19 Goads, with "on"
24 Finds fault
26 Fat forgoer of rhyme
29 Like bowl games
30 Beast of Borden
33 Labor leader Chavez
34 Of days gone by
35 Weak brew
36 Similar in sound
37 Former monetary unit of Madrid
38 Like some Poe poems
41 Rob Reiner's father
43 Face mask wearer
44 Stationary
45 Eyeglass pair
48 Gloomy, in poetry
50 Major suffix
52 H.S. junior's test
53 Ready and willing partner
56 Scratch (out)
57 VCRs' companions

ANSWER, PAGE 87

47

LEAVING LAS VEGAS

ACROSS

1 Rob once of "The West Wing"
5 Dull discomfort
9 Top dog
14 Infielder Rodriguez
15 Burro bellow
16 "Cold Mountain" star Zellweger
17 Bush ___ (Dubya's dad)
18 Arthurian era, e.g.
19 "Babalu" bandleader Desi
20 Steps done in sadness?
23 Refinable rock
24 Digits used when the IRS gets its hand in your pocket
25 Texas tea container
27 Pita treats
29 Flu fighters
31 George's lyrical brother
32 Pro ___ (for now)
34 "The X-Files" extras
35 Didn't just pass
36 Actor Dean with philosopher Thomas?
40 Makes a boo-boo
41 Back seat driver, e.g.
42 Pen end
43 NASA vehicle
44 Bit part for a star
46 One that eats shoots and leaves?
50 Sonic boom speed
52 Rd. map line
54 Bruin Hall of Famer Bobby
55 Electricity pioneer/battery namesake?
58 Debonair
59 "Laugh-In" regular Johnson
60 "It's not gonna happen"
61 Used a crowbar on
62 Well-honed
63 Lectern locale
64 Staten Island boat
65 "Calm down ..."
66 Elects (to)

DOWN

1 Cuddly pet
2 Owner of a barnburner?
3 Klemperer of "Hogan's Heroes"
4 VP, or some other VIP
5 Deep chasm
6 Queen toppers
7 Mata ___
8 Enamel-covered canine
9 Moves on all fours
10 King that met the Magi
11 Vampire chronicler
12 Parts of a score
13 Candy dispensed through a head
21 Krupp Works city
22 Makes a pass at
26 "Spy vs. Spy" mag
28 Elevator innovator
30 Use weasel words
33 Tomorrow, to Tomás
35 "Mamma Mia!" band
36 Word in many horror film titles
37 ___ quarterback
38 II, to I
39 Two-footed creature
40 Nightmare street of film
44 Dante wrote a divine one
45 Proclaims with pomp
47 "Fat chance!"
48 "Put the gun down!"
49 "Gunsmoke" star James
51 Hummingbirds do it
53 Itsy-bitsy
56 Carpeting measurement
57 Prefix with China
58 Lotion letters

ANSWER, PAGE 88

SOLE MUSIC

ACROSS

1 Hindu deity
5 Begin in earnest
10 "Promised Land" author
14 First name in pitching
15 Amazon activity, e.g.
16 "Cleopatra" backdrop
17 "Only Love Can Break a Heart" performer
19 Like much rush-hour traffic, ironically
20 How movers might move a sofa
21 Tiny tubes
23 Lao-tzu's system
24 Mice, to cats
25 Stuck on oneself
27 Acapulco auntie
28 Oliver Stone film
31 Hamburg's river
34 With 43-Across, "It's Only Make Believe" performer

36 Slangy intensifier
37 Shot in the dark
39 Mai ___ cocktail
40 Broccoli bit
42 Rap sheet abbr.
43 See 34-Across
46 "Now, Voyager" actress Chase
47 Mistletoe mo.
48 Article in Berlin
49 Work by Irving Berlin
51 End of the loaf
53 Go through again
57 Actor Jason of "Philadelphia"
60 Chalet environs
61 Story line
62 "We've Only Just Begun" performers, with "the"

64 Central American Native American
65 Rite site
66 "Bus Stop" playwright William
67 Pt. of DOS
68 Bursts at the seams
69 Scholarship basis, sometimes

DOWN

1 Word reference pioneer
2 Word before football
3 Bronson's "The Evil That ___"
4 Pub proprietresses
5 Pertaining to bad vibrations?
6 Ending for Ann

7 Catch some rays
8 Start of a Tony Orlando title
9 Dukakis of "Mr. Holland's Opus"
10 Follow
11 "Only the Good Die Young" performer
12 Lip balm ingredient
13 What papers carry
18 Tuscan tilting tower town
22 Earnestly hopes
26 Out to lunch, for example
27 Foolish folk
29 Antiaircraft fire
30 Supergirl's Krypton name
31 "Yipes!" of yore

32 Anakin Skywalker's son
33 "God Only Knows" performers
35 Singer ___ King Cole
38 Work the wheel
41 Kids' language
44 University of Kentucky athlete
45 New ___ (Big Apple residents)
50 Frankfort refusal
52 Bother a bunch
54 Ryan of "The Beverly Hillbillies"
55 On the ___ of (approaching)
56 Made bearable
57 Tach readings, for short
58 Word on a lotion bottle
59 Clearance event
60 Unwanted e-mail
63 Numbered hwy.

ANSWER, PAGE 91

49

FLIP-FLOP

ACROSS

1 "Beetle Bailey" character named for a Greek
6 Long pass
10 Do mouth-to-mouth recreation?
14 Didn't stop
15 Czech runner Zátopek
16 Netman Nastase
17 "___ having fun yet?"
18 Bancroft or Boleyn
19 Valuable vein
20 Flip
23 Prefix with cycle
24 Balm target
25 Suffix with Siam
26 Writer LeShan
28 Midterm, for example
30 Margot's "Superman" role
32 Boston boss, for example
34 Question source
36 As well
37 Flop
41 "Venus" singer Frankie
42 Our, in Tours
43 Mideast desert
44 Pop, in Paris
45 Old newspaper part
49 Hal Foster comic character
50 Congo's cont.
52 Pirate's interjections
54 Bath bathroom
55 Flip-flop
59 Marlon in "The Godfather"
60 Hockey nickname
61 Andes wool source
62 Think tank nugget
63 Knock for a loop
64 "Love Story" author Erich
65 "Over here!"
66 ___ Kong
67 Gladiator's domain

DOWN

1 Czech capital
2 Adam's apple locale
3 Absence of oomph
4 Minor municipality
5 Tatum of "Paper Moon"
6 Allen Ginsberg, for one
7 Science magazine
8 Chops finely
9 Grace word
10 Metric mass unit
11 Valentine words
12 Hasty exit site
13 "Told ya!"
21 Smooth and soft
22 Personal account
27 El Prado paintings, e.g.
29 Sap source
31 "Goodnight" gal of song
33 Better qualified
35 Language closely related to Czech
36 Spuds
37 Site where water became wine, some say
38 Errs on "The Price Is Right"
39 Captains of industry
40 Without spending much
44 "Voilà!"
46 It's "youthless"
47 Without exception
48 "Such lovely dancers!"
51 Blood partner
53 Tex-Mex condiment
56 Paint application
57 Imitated Rumpelstiltskin
58 N.Y. Met or L.A. Dodger, e.g.
59 Bigshot, briefly

ANSWER, PAGE 92

YOUR SOMETHING ELSE

ACROSS

1 Gulf War craft
6 Ending for ab or ad
10 Sound on a cobblestone street
14 Postgame summary
15 Pearl Harbor's island
16 Little-hand indication
17 Greta of "I vant to be alone" fame
18 Salt Lake City athletes
19 Off course
20 Your inns for sailors?
23 Touches with a baseball
24 Rubber stamps pound it
27 Impromptu bookmark
30 Winter product prefix, in ads
31 "Lord, is ___?"
32 Romeo's rival
33 CD, e.g.
35 Middle name of a rock 'n' roll legend
36 Your best buying opportunity?
39 Edinburgh native
40 Kill, as a bill
41 Path prefix
42 The Common Mkt.
43 Jazz guitarist Montgomery
44 Hideous her
46 Steerer of steers
48 Land map
49 Your conservative Brit's home?
55 Part of a stand-up routine
57 Ring around the moon
58 Title holder
59 Speed skater Heiden
60 Pancake topping
61 "___ c'est moi"
62 Trudge
63 Academic session
64 Quick Internet message

DOWN

1 Jason's craft
2 Teach to abstain
3 Plot piece
4 They get you off your feet and use meters
5 Unscientific survey
6 Disdain of the unattainable
7 Solemn pledges
8 Prefix with stat
9 Enter forcefully
10 Cue stick application
11 Depression
12 SOS part, supposedly
13 Get nosy
21 Travel org.
22 Rocker Brian
25 Makes up
26 Wild dog of the outback
27 Member of Santa's team
28 Black-and-white bite
29 Crux of the matter
30 Pedagogue's place
32 Sat, waiting for a click
34 Iowa hrs.
35 Cathedral nook
37 Went past
38 Window with an ocean view
43 On the small side
45 Like some holiday apparel
47 Sweater with a letter?
48 Gondola guy
50 Chaucer piece
51 Wilson of "Zoolander"
52 Passé preposition
53 Senate position
54 Art deco designer
55 Hot tub part
56 Bruins great Bobby

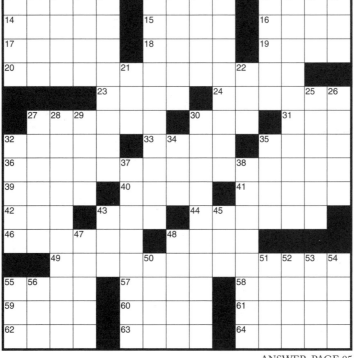

ANSWER, PAGE 95

SO TO SPEEK

ACROSS

1 Stargazers' bear
5 Looks like a lecher
10 Don of morning radio
14 Sanctuary furniture
15 Hosiery hue
16 Hockey venue
17 Voyeur's deed?
20 Sister of Zsa Zsa
21 Neighbor of Georgia and Turkey
22 Suffix with percent
23 Sell to the public
25 Ready to go
27 Get some onion from the cooler?
31 Arty New York neighborhood
33 Physics Nobelist Bohr
34 Feels poorly
37 Political party managers
39 Slippery swimmer
40 Earth Day month
41 Auto option, informally
42 Ruffle the feathers of
45 Oolong or Earl Grey, e.g.
46 Nobody at all
48 Discusses enthusiastically
50 "Make my day, mailman!"
51 ___ alai
52 Seven days of cattiness?
59 ___ dancer
60 Try to bite, puppy-style
61 Red Sea port
63 Asian inland sea
64 News analyst Van Susteren
65 Harvester's haul
66 Sanford portrayer Foxx
67 Winding road features
68 ___ Kong

DOWN

1 Word before crust or hand
2 Superman portrayer Christopher
3 Workout wear
4 One way to find out
5 College near Cleveland
6 Antibiotic target
7 Biographical focus
8 "Ghostbusters" character
9 Soap operas, for example
10 "The Stepford Wives" author Levin
11 Garments that show a lot of leg
12 Title for Sam of government
13 Sport with clay pigeons
18 Low poker hand
19 Stag or bull, e.g.
24 Each, in pricing
26 Word before year
28 Dorothy, to Em
29 Dork
30 Divvy up
31 Adult ugly duckling
32 John Glenn's state
35 In ___ of
36 Sharp rebuke
38 Proverbial baby deliverer
40 Black key above G
43 Close enough to hit
44 Tex-Mex treats
47 From long ago
49 Fuzzy dice and such
52 Became threadbare
53 "Omigosh!"
54 Round Table sitters
55 King Kong and kin
56 Winslet of "Eternal Sunshine of the Spotless Mind"
57 Prefix with dollar
58 Brightly colored
59 Needle-nosed fish
62 Fam. planning goal

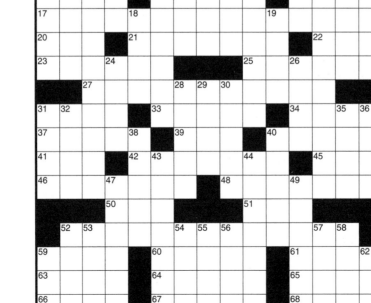

ANSWER, PAGE 96

IN THE SHORT RUN

ACROSS

1 Monastery man
5 Table salt, to a chemist
9 Licorice flavoring
14 Monastery image
15 Feature of an empty house
16 "Divine Comedy" poet
17 Judi Dench, for one
18 Start of a riddle
20 Most similar to the Sahara
22 Porter's regretful Miss
23 Mil. drop site
24 Newscaster Ellerbee
25 Thespian area
26 Obsolete map abbr.
27 Aunt in "Bambi"
28 "I Shot Andy Warhol" star Taylor
30 Stick ___ in the water
31 More of the riddle
36 Single-named supermodel
37 La ___ Tar Pits
38 End of the riddle
44 Rover's reward
45 Archer with wings
46 Whirlpool site
47 "Andy Capp" cartoonist Smythe
48 Attraction near Orlando
51 Worry greatly
53 Cola cooler
54 Vault
55 Not on the level
56 Answer to the riddle
59 Cake part
60 Barely making, with "out"
61 Light weight
62 Humorous Bombeck
63 Tooth trouble
64 Leg up
65 Use a sickle, say

DOWN

1 40th key on a piano keyboard
2 Egg-shaped instrument
3 Trifling
4 Hit with a joint
5 "Macbeth" eye donor?
6 Oberhausen outburst
7 In disarray
8 Led Zeppelin's "Whole ___ Love"
9 Give ___ of one's own medicine
10 Rebellion leader Turner
11 Lickety-split
12 Blended family member
13 Pooh's pessimistic pal
19 Unkind remark
21 Deli dangler
25 Colorful talk
29 Caspian Sea land
30 Asian nurse
32 Not recorded
33 Movie critic Roger
34 Estimate ending
35 Admits, with "up"
38 Bread once baked on a farm tool
39 Like Nativity fliers
40 Cat with spots
41 Fred of "Top Hat"
42 Famed Rio beach
43 Ramshackle structure
44 Greased the palm of
48 Lyric lamentation
49 Part of RPM
50 Bum off of
52 Take in or let out
55 Quaint sigh
57 Type of forensic evidence
58 Mattress problem

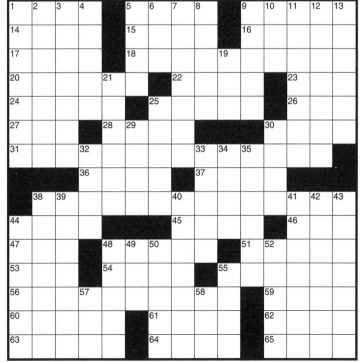

ANSWER, PAGE 81

COMPARATIVELY SPEAKING

ACROSS

1 Madras mister
6 Scotch servings
11 Parasite's home
15 Popeye's gal
16 Touch base
17 Spillane's "___ Jury"
18 Rash
21 Titans' org.
22 "The Sonnets to Orpheus" poet
23 Supermarket tabloid bits, often
24 Buns and beehives
25 Italian wine center
26 Holm of "All About Eve"
27 Executive, slangily

29 Handle the helm
31 Costner character
32 Make a minister of
35 What cleats increase
37 Rasher
43 Bela's role in "Son of Frankenstein"
44 Get testy with
46 Cable syst.
50 Rosemary and thyme, e.g.
53 Wannabe rock star's tape
54 Sets straight
56 Bit to split
59 St. Peter's fishing gear
60 Bit of bait
61 String section member

62 Controvertial bug killer
63 Rashest
66 Frasier's response to a client
67 Man of morals
68 Millionaire on the Titanic
69 Spilled the beans
70 Brings up
71 Stairway parts

DOWN

1 Some #@%*& individual
2 Hands and knees
3 Ski run spot
4 Direct ending
5 Oft-quoted Yogi
6 Poles with footrests
7 Cope, slangily
8 Shrek, for one
9 Mon. follower

10 Rack on a barbecue, maybe
11 Underworld figures
12 Idle
13 Minimovies
14 Tightens up
19 WWII group
20 ___-de-sac
26 "What's My Line" panelist Bennett
28 Sea dog
30 Freudian concern
33 Campus climber
34 P.J.'s, e.g.
36 Harsh review
38 Thumbs-down reactions
39 "That makes me mad!"
40 Dirtbag

41 Part of a flexible schedule
42 Pretend to know important people
45 Walks with a wobble
46 Pledge
47 Melodic passage
48 Metallic Christmas tree decoration
49 Blew off steam
51 One who deals with a bondsman
52 Defeats decisively
55 Doze off
57 Schnozz add-on
58 American pyramid builders
61 Credit card kind
64 Neckline type
65 OK clock setting

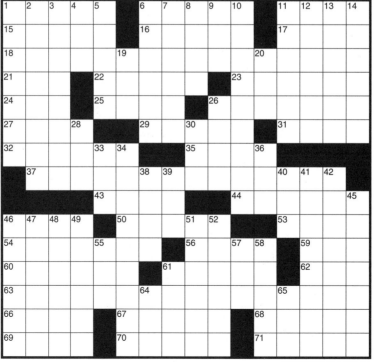

ANSWER, PAGE 82

AIRPORT HOTEL

ACROSS

1 Catches on to
5 Take the wheel
10 Needing a whirlpool, perhaps
14 Foolhardy
15 Sandra Bullock's "___ You Were Sleeping"
16 Gin flavor
17 Memo start
18 Check the books
19 Helpful hints
20 Novel about the pharmacy industry
23 "The Republic" author
24 "Star Trek" actor Spiner who played Data
25 Corp. cash handler
27 Maple fluid
28 Frequently, in poetry
30 With 42-Across, author of "Airport," "Hotel," and three novels in this puzzle
32 Archie and Edith, to Mike
35 Pickled delicacies
36 Novel about banks, with "The"
40 Dentist's office call
41 German chancellor Adenauer
42 See 30-Across
45 Notebook divider label
46 Time-out for tots
49 Old Ford model
50 Country singer Carter
53 Carol opening
55 Novel about hospitals, with "The"
58 Italian side dish
59 "... ___ man put asunder"
60 Alpine sight
61 Get rid of, with "out"
62 Prudential rival
63 Stake driver
64 Untouchable chief
65 Error's partner
66 Basilica section

DOWN

1 Catches on to
2 Cheech Marin movie locale
3 Woman's shoe feature
4 "I'm all ears"
5 Plunder, slangily
6 Bulletin sticker
7 Sort of down
8 Say "nothin'," e.g.
9 Blind spot's location
10 Vino venue
11 Decisive statement
12 Promising people
13 "Oui," when we say it
21 '60s pop star Peter
22 Community bldg.
26 Surgery sites, for short
29 Birds do it
31 Angry, with "off"
32 Like many JFK flights
33 One of the five W's
34 Mexican general at the Alamo
36 Like a vegetarian diet
37 Gets rusty, e.g.
38 New Deal inits.
39 Libreville's land
40 Rinks org.
43 Child expert LeShan
44 Address loudly
46 "You're out of luck"
47 Near miss, for a valedictorian
48 Pharmacist's grinder
51 "Doe, ___ ..." (lyric from "The Sound of Music")
52 Sicilian gangster Frank
54 Curve that gives one pause?
56 Silent assents
57 Hamm score
58 Part of MYOB

ANSWER, PAGE 85

55

LIE IN WAIT

ACROSS

1 Invader of Iberia
5 Tattered attire
9 Dangle a carrot in front of
14 Alice's Restaurant patron
15 Goofing off
16 Battery part
17 Film winds up on it
18 Curmudgeon
19 Italian bridge
20 Send some cads to the Arctic?
23 Bonkers
24 Potatoes au ___
27 Leaning
30 Convenient enc.
31 Carbon compound suffix
32 Do acupuncture here and there?
35 Label for Elvis
36 Carried away
37 Goof
38 "Cat on ___ Tin Roof"
39 Sweetie
40 Serve on a magazine's softball team?
44 They round up AWOLs
45 Descartes's conclusion
46 Miss a step
47 Give out
49 Make a face smoother
51 Steal seconds?
56 Orange container
58 New Mexico native
59 Joel or Jennifer
60 Gemstone weight
61 Party to
62 Emperor of old
63 Game of bishops and knights
64 Lose control on ice
65 Fast also-ran

DOWN

1 Latin singer Anthony
2 Chocolate sandwich
3 Stick in the dairy case
4 Return to a lower level
5 Lasagna ingredient
6 One score after deuce
7 "Mine eyes have seen the ___ ..."
8 Son of Adam and Eve
9 Coming to a point
10 Name on a bomber
11 Huge success on Broadway
12 LAX clock setting
13 Comfy shirt
21 Soldier in "Over There"
22 Richard of "A Summer Place"
25 What one makes
26 Less cluttered
27 Breathing woe
28 Front porches
29 Disproportionately large portion
30 Wander around the Web
33 Paper quantity
34 "Kid" of the jazz trombone
38 On and on
40 Small swine
41 Hit the beach
42 Inclined
43 Beatle George's sitarist friend
48 Tiny amounts
49 Gumption
50 Vietnam's capital
52 Commando weapons
53 Word in two constellation names
54 Cheek dampener
55 "Jane ___"
56 New Deal prog.
57 When repeated, enthusiastic

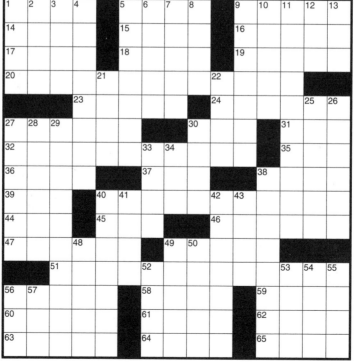

ANSWER, PAGE 86

THE END OF THE LINE

ACROSS

1 George of "Where's Poppa?"
6 Spitballs, e.g.
10 Smart-___
14 ___ Ingalls Wilder
15 Film follower?
16 Word after pro
17 Garrick ___ (first on-site reporter of the Vietnam War)
18 Urban locale of the church of 34-Across
20 Where Old Man River makes his deposits?
21 Collection of brains
22 Sign of a hit
23 Team for which 34-Across played
25 Pie-in-the-face sound
27 N.C. hrs.
28 Finless fish
29 Get off on the tarmac
31 Club with clubs in its logo: Abbr.
32 Go, with "on down"
33 "Them" insects
34 Retired NFL lineman who inspired this puzzle
37 What some writers work on
39 Inc., in England
40 Hosp. workers
41 Like a car full of money
43 Stylish, in the '60s
44 FBI guy
47 Unwanted sound
48 With 55-Across, nickname of 34-Across
50 Voight of "Zoolander"
51 Walt Disney's middle name
54 John Hancock rival
55 See 48-Across
57 Like some college walls
58 Person of vision
59 "Firebird" composer Stravinsky
60 "You've got some ___!"
61 Current awhirl
62 Current producers
63 Work with the hands

DOWN

1 Drain blocker
2 Dreamers, to lotus flowers
3 Throat
4 Mountain ridge
5 Die on the stage
6 ___ magnetism
7 Bank contents
8 Ont. neighbor
9 Metal-bearing minerals
10 Start of a kindergarten song
11 Teri Hatcher's role in "Lois & Clark: The New Adventures of Superman"
12 Contest competitor
13 Wile E. et al.
19 Speak like a tough guy
24 Snoopy, for one
26 Land maps
29 Wall Street barometer, with "the"
30 "You've Got Mail" director Nora
31 New Mexico river
32 Four-poster, e.g.
34 Prompted
35 "___ be a pleasure!"
36 Lettering liquid
37 "Do You Know the Way to ___"
38 Examined for flaws
42 Coral habitat
43 Scrooge and Silas Marner, e.g.
44 Dress code concern
45 League of Nations home
46 Bought and sold
48 TV lawyer Perry
49 "Magnificent" movie number
52 Mariner Ericson
53 "Young Frankenstein" role
56 Suffix with trick

ANSWER, PAGE 89

57

HO AND MO'

ACROSS

1 English channel nickname, with "the"
5 Drive-thru banks
9 Wide-open
14 Trout tempter
15 When repeated, a child's train
16 "American Idol" winner Studdard
17 Lake of Commodore Perry's victory
18 Sounds of disapproval
19 Man with the golden touch?
20 Ho
23 Belgrade resident
24 Famous last words
25 Orzo or ziti, e.g.
28 "In Search of ..." host Leonard
31 Lucy's sidekick
32 "Buyer beware" warning
33 Air pollution
37 Ho Ho
40 Polio vaccine developer
41 Toward shelter
42 Corrode
43 Topples from power
44 Cries from a donkey
45 Pie fight sound effects
49 Package carrier
51 "Ho, ho, ho!"
57 Have one's say
58 Comical Carvey
59 Steel or virgin follower
60 Track transaction
61 Olympic medalist Louganis
62 "Thanks ___!"
63 Like the Family Robinson
64 Freedom from concern
65 Singer Ono

DOWN

1 Ran in the wash
2 Mark replacer
3 Wilde country
4 Hearty entree
5 Cast member
6 Rough sketches, or polished surfaces
7 It may eat your shorts
8 Nothing special
9 National Guard center
10 Cunning
11 Former "American Idol" judge Paula
12 Loud bursts
13 Go after
21 Bailiwick
22 Lasso loop
25 Bodybuilder's pride
26 Big name in razors
27 "A Boy Named Sue" writer Silverstein
29 Spot in the water
30 Major events
33 Cause to lose courage
34 ___ Hari of espionage
35 Pretty good
36 Hears clearly
38 Legendary soul-seller
39 Items in red
43 2001 Nicole Kidman film, with "The"
45 Brakes
46 Melonlike fruit
47 One of the Mario Brothers
48 Endora portrayer, on "Bewitched"
50 No longer a minor
52 Upper hand
53 Avis adjective
54 Legal plea, for short
55 Ripped off
56 Low-voiced lady

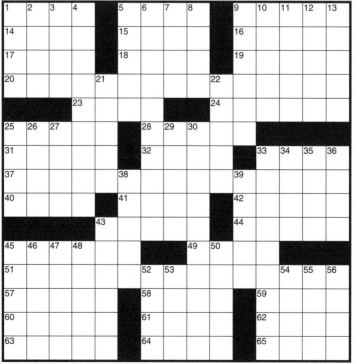

ANSWER, PAGE 90

ARTICLE REWRITTEN

ACROSS
1 O.K. Corral gunfighter
5 Much-visited place
10 ___ homo
14 High spirits
15 Community character
16 Draw two lines through
17 Italian sports car, for short
18 Matter makers
19 Corp. VIP
20 Coats with burnt color?
23 Unbending
24 Sit before a lens
25 Not masc.
28 Simon or Diamond
30 Former language columnist William
32 Close call at the barbershop?
37 Hate the thought of
38 [I'm in trouble!]
39 Puts out
41 Additional
42 "Put two and two together," for one
44 New recipe?
46 Hard to move
48 Fuddy-duddy
49 Snaky shape
50 Insurer's assessment
53 Stick like glue
57 Go skating?
60 Standing on
62 Warm, in a way
63 Deal with it
64 "Lady Jane Grey" writer Nicholas
65 Talk show host Degeneres
66 Together, in music
67 "Jurassic Park" threat, briefly
68 Palindromic court star
69 Crunch counts

DOWN
1 Word of mock horror
2 Pass out
3 Send, as to a specialist
4 Well-matched pair
5 Intervening stretch
6 Part of Caesar's last question
7 Munch noisily
8 Small band
9 Take stock of
10 Really big show
11 "Hee Haw" setting
12 Stick on a table
13 "Independence Day" attackers
21 Skillful server
22 Part of ROM
26 Tape over
27 Jason's wife
29 Peru's capital
31 Train part without passengers
32 Quick-thinking
33 Michelangelo's "David," and others
34 Sewing machine inventor
35 Confession topic
36 Blended-family prefix
40 Crusaders' foes
43 Griffin of game shows
45 Lunar effect
47 Sisters' daughters
51 French explorer La ___
52 Mound
54 Lose ground?
55 Turn into confetti
56 Olympic weapons
58 High point
59 Chin stroker's words
60 Gallery objects
61 Rocky projection

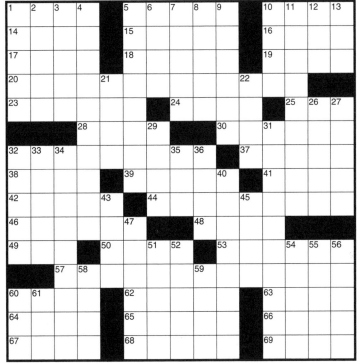

ANSWER, PAGE 93

59

EMPLOYEE-EMPLOYER RELATIONSHIP

ACROSS

1 Flyers with narrow waists
6 Follows persistently
10 Penelope of "Vanilla Sky"
14 Words before "Fine" and "Pretty," in song
15 Windows' picture
16 Sighed aside
17 Start to pop?
18 Defeat in a yelling match
20 Money chest full of java?
22 Non-Rx
23 Carrier to Oslo
24 Word before door or poodle
28 They may be wild or rolled
30 Rice University athletes
32 Suffix with press
33 "___! Went the Strings of My Heart"
35 Cosmetics compound?
38 Performed on stage
40 The other woman
41 Fought the clock
42 French chef's knife?
45 Ticks off
46 Mideast gp.
47 Prefix with care or kit
48 Cooking vessel
50 Out in left field
52 Test for college srs.
53 Chi. clock setting
56 One who pulls Jeter from the lineup?
60 Just lose it
63 Down on one's luck
64 Sarcastic response
65 Drink served over cracked ice
66 Wears down
67 ___ trap
68 Suffix with leather
69 Advent

DOWN

1 "Roger, ___!"
2 What the game is, according to Holmes
3 Inner strength
4 Ill-gotten gain
5 Most cunning
6 They go into drives
7 ___ Rios, Jamaica
8 Blunder
9 Sound heard in hay fever season
10 Core group
11 Greek consonant
12 Underground org.
13 "Moment of ___" (feature of "The Daily Show")
19 More to the point
21 Maneuver slowly
25 What the Rockettes dress up as during the holidays
26 Word after Battle, in Michigan
27 Buffalo bunches
29 "A Death in the Family" author James
30 Cheri of "Saturday Night Live"
31 Used to be
33 Rock artist Frank
34 Poker declaration
36 Roe source
37 Travel smoothly
39 Take down a peg
43 Love handle?
44 Calhoun of "The Texan"
49 Rough house
51 First name in Tombstone lore
52 Romantic adventure
54 "Fiddle-___!"
55 Lovers' lane event
57 Make a sweater, perhaps
58 All-star game side, often
59 "No," in Nuremberg
60 Bellows of "Ally McBeal"
61 "Shogun" sash
62 Stiller of "Meet the Fockers"

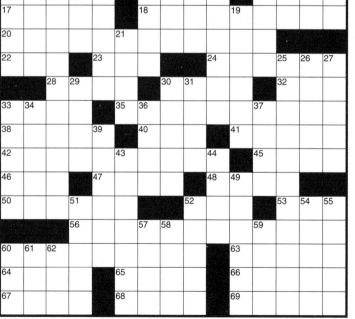

ANSWER, PAGE 94

MOTH MENU

ACROSS

1 Baldwin of "The SpongeBob SquarePants Movie"
5 Specter of government
10 Trucker with a handle
14 Game on horseback
15 Words before evil
16 Russian saint
17 Honolulu's location
18 Oktoberfest souvenir
19 Keyboard instrument
20 Tuxedos
23 Tropical root
24 Salon creation
25 Trip up a mountain
28 Norman who wrote "The Executioner's Song"
32 Fearful feline actor Bert
33 Country towers
37 Pro follower
38 Hog the stage
40 "Oh, brother!"
41 College course, briefly
42 Felt headwear
45 Magazine thickeners
47 Winter wind
48 Yuletide worker of myth
51 Crooner Cole
52 Juan's that
53 Altar in the sky
54 Ending with law or saw
55 Off the mark
57 German name connector
59 Mural artist Rivera
61 Close-fitting evening garments
64 Like a moonless night
65 Archipelago part
66 Neighbor of Ida.
67 Monster's loch
68 Duane ___ (drugstore chain)
69 Line segment extremes

DOWN

1 Letters on letters to GIs
2 Unit of laundry
3 Precollege
4 Against
5 States confidently
6 Fashionably nostalgic
7 Cobb of "12 Angry Men"
8 Digital dinosaur
9 Sarges, e.g.
10 Be of primary importance
11 Rorschach image
12 Swelled heads
13 Tabloid
21 Palindromic Bobbsey
22 Optima maker
25 Malt drink
26 Fictional detective Spade
27 Rookie piano piece
29 Takes a gander at
30 List abbr.
31 Stadium noise
34 Make it up as you go
35 Milk of Cannes
36 How to drive with an arm around a date
39 Papa Hemingway
41 Event with floats
43 WBO wins
44 Part of HRH
45 Excedrin competitor
46 Singer Vic
49 Map feature
50 Makes translucent
56 "The ___ the limit!"
58 Chili container
60 Words after "woe"
62 "Give me ___!" ("Stand back!")
63 AAA way

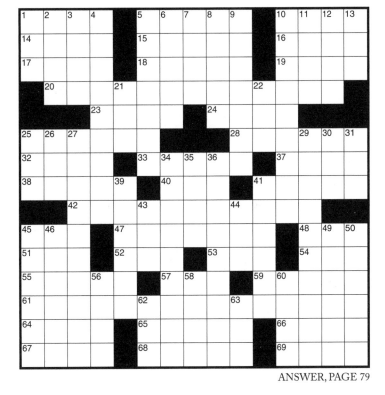

ANSWER, PAGE 79

GEOMETRIC RELATIONSHIPS

ACROSS

1 Decide with a coin
5 Jazz genre
10 Hot tubs
14 Capable of
15 Become accustomed
16 Outstanding
17 Reiner of "Dead Men Don't Wear Plaid"
18 Prescribed amounts
19 "Heinz 57 varieties" dog
20 Person you can trust
23 Postal scale units
24 English county
27 Region around Beersheba
28 Naturally occurring potassium nitrate
32 Put on the payroll
34 Conch shell effect
35 Group you can trust
40 Butter alternative
41 Less imaginative
42 Trims
44 More likely to mouth off
49 Surveil, with "out"
50 Closing number
51 Relationships with people you can't trust
56 Defender of rts.
58 Long piano
59 Turn in chess
60 Browning of pages of verse, for example
61 Model soldier?
62 Sherman Hemsley religious sitcom
63 Drops the curtain on
64 Reaches across
65 Money given from Lucy to Ethel

DOWN

1 Arizona metropolis
2 Hard to understand
3 Kept waiting, with "along"
4 Comfort in sorrow
5 ___ one's time (waits)
6 Grandson of Eve
7 Type of league
8 After-lunch sandwich
9 Colombian coin
10 Me-tooism phrase
11 Increase the intensity
12 Aardvark's tidbit
13 Part of a musical gig
21 Whoop it up
22 Cooking meas.
25 "___ my lips!"
26 Misses the mark
28 Wear with pride
29 Role for Jude or Michael
30 Spots for choirs
31 British wheel
33 Prefix with physical
35 Types of Atlantic fish
36 "Before ___ you go ..."
37 Brought back to the factory, say
38 Meals eaten in the open
39 Apollo 15 astronaut James
43 MLK's title
45 Director Bergman
46 She danced for Herod
47 Time for an early lunch
48 Take offense at
50 Loses brightness
52 They go with bacon
53 Send sprawling
54 Indian chief
55 "Can I get ___ this?"
56 Musclebound brute
57 Debate side

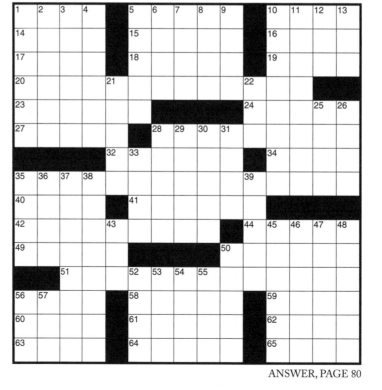

ANSWER, PAGE 80

ARTIFICIAL GREENERY

ACROSS

1 Where not to throw bouquets, in a song
5 "You said it!"
9 Grass-skirt dances
14 Experience shame
16 Send to seventh heaven
17 Dynamic Duo wheels
18 "Giant" of wrestling
19 Carry grass clippings?
21 "Caught you!"
22 "I'm Sorry" singer Brenda
23 Outfielder's throw, maybe
24 Singer-turned-politician Sonny
26 Salon strokes
29 DDE's arena
30 Genial sort
32 "Peachy!"
35 Nothing but foliage?
39 Rust or lime, e.g.
40 Kathleen Turner's "___ Sue Got Married"
43 Slalom segment
46 Prey on the mind of
49 Ice house: Var.
50 Infomercial imperative
53 Eyeball or Earth, e.g.
55 Wheaton of "Stand by Me"
56 Upright twigs?
60 Namely
61 Roman Catholic liturgy
63 France's longest river
64 "Outta bed!"
65 Make changes to
66 Turns to the right
67 Cowardly Lion player Lahr

DOWN

1 Mil. jet locale
2 Coffeehouse alternative
3 Antifreeze additive
4 Giggling Muppet
5 Strolls leisurely
6 Word before name or voyage
7 She, in Vichy
8 Cub or Brave, for short
9 Makes sound?
10 Arm bones
11 Edinburgh boy
12 Motionless
13 Takes care of
15 ___ mate
20 Metabolism descriptor
21 Crunch targets
25 Two-toned snack
27 Map legend, usually
28 Princess insomnia source
31 Uncle Sam's take
33 Go over
34 The Shirelles' "Dedicated to the ___ Love"
36 Looks at
37 Author LeShan
38 Meringue ingredient
41 Seem to be gold, perhaps
42 Deborah's costar in "The King and I"
43 So. California city
44 Nine-month interruption of summer vacation?
45 "Say no more!"
47 Major blood vessels
48 Gets in shape
51 Bête ___
52 Web-footed mammal
54 Tie up
57 Powerful punch
58 Sticky 3M product
59 Seize
62 Ambulance VIP

ANSWER, PAGE 83

63

WHERE OFF

ACROSS

1 Fabled race loser
5 Boxes with bows, usually
10 Scratching post users
14 Tributes in verse
15 French farewell
16 Old Italian money
17 Back muscles, briefly
18 Of the kidneys
19 Opera feature
20 Where to find one's shadow?
22 Think obsessively
23 "The Raven" monogram
24 Catherine ___-Jones
25 Positive aspect
27 "No need to explain"
29 ___ avis

31 One of the Three Stooges
32 Bloodhound's asset
33 Where to spank a comic?
35 Chimp in space
38 Cave ricochet
39 Where to find a lawyer?
43 Yell from a roller coaster
47 Start of the work wk.
48 Cartoon skunk Le Pew
49 Stool pigeon
51 Actress Plummer
53 James of "Misery"
55 U-turn from SSW
56 Leslie Caron role

57 Where a bachelor hangs out?
60 Concerning
61 Golfer with an army
62 Swanky
63 Country singer McCoy
64 Absolute, as nonsense
65 Treble clef singer
66 Emerald and diamond, e.g.
67 Inventor Nikola
68 ___ point

DOWN

1 German painter Hans
2 In the very recent past
3 Does over, as a manuscript

4 Gas brand in Canada
5 Small attic
6 That is
7 Painting or sculpture, e.g.
8 Dark greenish blue
9 Kind of acid
10 School group
11 Broadcast hour
12 Checked for fit
13 Kelp, e.g.
21 Israeli machine gun
26 Course of action
28 "Boston Public" extra
30 ___ bit (slightly)
33 Rush job letters
34 Scattered, as seed
36 "Hill Street Blues" org.

37 Undersea explorer
39 Picturing in the mind
40 Convention's choice
41 What "evil" is to "vile"
42 Certain trigonometric ratios
44 Harrison Ford's "Star Wars" role
45 Carmaker Maserati
46 Optical range
49 Tourist's take-along
50 Darth, as a boy
52 What a Bohr!
54 Shakespearean spirit
58 One-named designer
59 Hit with unwanted messages

ANSWER, PAGE 84

SINGER'S RANGE

ACROSS

1 Carbo-loader's fare
6 Drinks like a dog
10 Hammered obliquely
14 Where you first kiss your spouse
15 Eight, in Ecuador
16 Minestrone morsels
17 Like Leif
18 Long, long time
19 Prefix with scope
20 On the range, the singer cooks pancakes ___ ...
23 Tom and Sid, to Twain
24 By word of mouth
25 Big Apple area
27 Tibetans and Thais, e.g.
31 Oliver Twist, for one
35 Miserably moist
37 Ice house
38 ... carrots ___ ...
41 Weariness
42 Ted Kennedy's daughter
43 Christmas poem opener
44 Snooping (around)
46 Hair wave
48 Gold medalist Lipinski
50 "Sweet home" of song and cinema
55 ... and tofu ___
59 Wife of Zeus
60 Third place
61 Lott of Mississippi
62 Welcome post-accident words
63 Glinda portrayer in "The Wiz"
64 Get the graphite out
65 Fan mag
66 1914 Belgian battle line
67 Pill dispenser

DOWN

1 Huffs and puffs
2 Polynesian greeting
3 Soda insert
4 Nice to nosh
5 Rugged ridges
6 Usurer
7 Got 100 on
8 ID item
9 Northwest Mexican state
10 Highest level
11 City on the Oka
12 Pound of poetry books
13 "Go ahead!"
21 Wear away
22 Foundation
26 From the keg
28 "There oughta be ___!"
29 "Brothers & Sisters" mother
30 Bread pieces, to fondue
31 Austria's capital, to Austrians
32 Part of A.D.
33 Charged particles
34 Eccentric
36 "M*A*S*H" setting
39 "I've Been Working on the Railroad" woman
40 Rhea's "Cheers" role
45 Frightful
47 Like hard-to-comb hair
49 Hearth heap
51 Pack animal
52 Geometry calculations
53 Parson's place
54 Change, as a hemline
55 Virtuoso
56 Prefix meaning "half"
57 Hulks pump it
58 Topnotch

ANSWER, PAGE 87

YOU CAN SAY THAT AGAIN

ACROSS

1 Buster Brown's dog
5 Man of words William
11 "Now!" in a hospital
15 Soon, to Shakespeare
16 Lots of lions
17 Groaned refusal
18 Word after American
19 Come unglued
20 Cold-blooded, warm-hearted cartoon pet
21 Unyielding singer?
24 East or West archipelago
25 Throat extract, at times
27 39, in a typical Jack Benny skit
28 Dismissive remark
33 Shift, tab, or enter, e.g.
34 Stands for
36 ___ contendere
37 Comparatively cunning
39 Folk singer Woody's son
40 Alternative to publish
42 Generous phrase
43 Prosecuting lawyer Bara?
46 Heavenly streaker
49 Decaying metal
53 Eggs, scientifically
54 Flat-changer's tool
59 Cryptographic org.
60 Get to the bottom of
62 Bullets and cannonballs, e.g.
63 Divided into lots
65 Bitter baseball player?
68 Burl of "Cat on a Hot Tin Roof"
69 Having goose pimples
70 Turned right
71 Sign away
72 "You don't say!"
73 Concerning

DOWN

1 Figure skater Babilonia
2 At risk
3 Lot
4 China's Zhou ___
5 Swimming pool sound
6 Memphis-born star's middle name
7 Punch deliverer
8 Something to think about
9 "American Pie" actress Tara
10 What the heirs split
11 Khartoum's country
12 Extreme sensitivity to criticism
13 Baum guardian
14 In spite of, in short
22 Litter noise
23 Rolling stone's lack, they say
24 Title words before "Camera" or "Rock"
26 Apollo played it
29 Like a line, for short
30 Wife of Mr. Dithers
31 Hit the ground
32 Hebrew "beginning"
35 Quick message
38 Fill with bullets
40 Prefix with scope
41 Military medal recipient
44 Monopoly holding
45 "Who's the Boss?" costar
46 Tile arrangement
47 Change gradually
48 Spilled the beans
50 Some bellybuttons
51 Group of discussion groups
52 Got by
55 Took to be booked
56 Fix, as text
57 PR concern
58 Actress Esther
61 Ming artifact
64 Korbut on the beam
66 "Lord, is ___?"
67 English dramatist Thomas

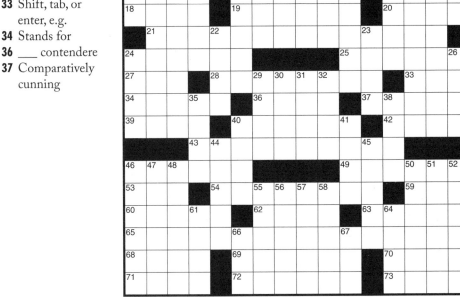

ANSWER, PAGE 88

WHAT HAPPENED WHEN ...

ACROSS

1 Lacking life
6 End of Caesar's claim
10 Suit ___
14 Ease off
15 James Dean or Marilyn Monroe, e.g.
16 Minnesota neighbor
17 ... George swore at that woman?
20 "Don't go away!"
21 Singer Etheridge
22 Leveling wedge
24 Greeting to Maria?
25 ... Tibbs longed for that woman?
33 Beach near Utah
34 Revivalists
35 Biblical Samuel's mentor
36 Mexican mint product
37 Pretend
39 Like some eagles
40 All-purpose vehicle, for short
41 Frisbee, for one
42 Newscaster Couric
43 ... a minister went by that woman?
47 January, in some dates
48 Unstable particle
49 Many homecoming attendees
53 "No, No, ___"
58 ... Keaton transported that woman?
60 Words before many words
61 Language-neutral puzzle
62 Miss America accessory
63 Full gestation period
64 Blue funk
65 Royal family VIPs

DOWN

1 Hoover and Electrolux, for short
2 Share a border with
3 Part of a Hispanic "What's up?"
4 ___-bitty
5 Far offshore
6 Murder mystery nonsurvivor
7 "ER" setting
8 Ending with micro or macro
9 Like apples during the fall
10 Neatened
11 Covetous coos
12 Knocks for a loop
13 Film plantation
18 German industrial area
19 Fairy tale shoemaker's helpers
23 Small video recorder
25 Finish off, as operations
26 "___ man with seven wives"
27 Enclosures with mss.
28 Howe'er
29 Piece of the whole: Abbr.
30 Actor Ledger of "Brokeback Mountain"
31 J.R. Ewing's mother
32 Bill attachment
37 Rifle and pistol
38 Second sight, for short
39 Slang for "good," ironically
41 "Death Be Not Proud" poet John
42 Branagh of "Wild Wild West"
44 Drum set component
45 End of day
46 In order (to)
49 Somewhat
50 Debussy's "Clair de ___"
51 SALT signatory
52 Israel's Abba
54 Falco of "The Sopranos"
55 Indochina native
56 Okla., once
57 Significant periods
59 Dangerous sprayer

ANSWER, PAGE 91

WITH A HEAVY HEART

ACROSS

1 Word before reader or tree
5 Highlander
9 Birthday treats
14 Out of action
15 Columnist Chase
16 On one's toes
17 Marquee filler
18 Follow furtively
19 E-mail option
20 Policeman of comedy
23 Cowboy sobriquet
24 Puts the collar on?
25 Replay option
27 ___ bean
29 Pilotless planes
32 Sugarcane cutters
36 By the book
37 Baseball family name
38 It means nothing
40 4,047 square meters
41 ___ paper (chemical indicator)
44 Share quarters
47 Ricky Martin, for one
48 Former Bruin Phil, to fans
49 Ignominy
51 Prima ballerinas
56 2,000 pounds, and word in the center of this puzzle's theme answers
58 1996 ticket
60 Non-Hispanic, in Hidalgo
62 Stretched out
63 Sea bordering Kazakhstan
64 Video game creator Sid
65 VIP vehicle
66 Arrangement holder
67 Start a closeup shot
68 Didst kill
69 Past partners

DOWN

1 Left-winger, in slang
2 "Doe, ___ ..."
3 Bentsen of "You're no Jack Kennedy" fame
4 Smart set
5 "Button your lip!"
6 Male Highlanders
7 Longhorn rival, in the NCAA
8 Spills the beans
9 Mustang's shelter
10 Beverage in a schooner
11 Held in reserve
12 First name in mystery writing
13 Underworld river
21 Mosaic piece
22 Part of REO
26 Fable feature
28 Half of a 45
30 Neutral shade
31 Twelfth of the AA program
32 Retail complex
33 Others, to Ovid
34 Southern seed remover
35 Like a rainforest
39 Fall behind
42 Mythical equine
43 ___ food
45 So far
46 Benefit
50 Paper producers and pepper grinders, e.g.
52 "___ at the office"
53 Ecologically minded Seuss creature
54 Clean blackboards
55 Monica of the court
56 Pack down
57 Top draft level
59 Catch red-handed
61 Island garland

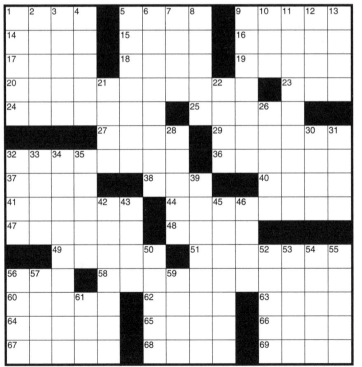

ANSWER, PAGE 92

TWO WEEKS' NOTICE

ACROSS

1 Papa's mate
5 Torch job
10 Recipe amt.
14 The Bard's river
15 Meeting request
16 Winter coating
17 "It's a deal!"
18 Diviner's deck
19 With skill
20 Poorly tied tie?
23 Fannie follower
24 "The Raven" writer
25 Peeper protector
27 Alex's mom on "Family Ties"
29 Fanatical
32 Chemical suffix
33 Danger to divers
35 Highway hauler
36 Had no doubt
37 Laid-back Native Americans?
41 Daddy-o
42 "Is that so!"
43 Afternoon social
44 Mother without a mother
45 Hunky-dory
47 Filled with wonder
51 Morning bowlful
53 That, in Tijuana
55 Proverbial amount of bricks
56 Opera, to its detractors?
60 Townshend of the Who
61 Killer whale at SeaWorld
62 Word between in and of
63 Foot offense, or polecat defense
64 Euripides tragedy
65 Chimney channel
66 Rocky peaks
67 Biased viewpoint
68 Sight from Salzburg

DOWN

1 Title for Tussaud
2 Frank admission
3 '60s dance
4 Over
5 Elroy's pooch
6 Bookworm
7 Romanian's neighbor
8 Melville sea tale
9 Measure of the contents
10 Macbeth's title
11 North American songbird
12 You can crumble them into soup
13 Ask too many questions
21 Sneak ___
22 "The Spanish Tragedy" dramatist
26 Drops on the ground?
28 Plies a needle
30 Packing heat
31 Life story, for short
34 Lawyer's terms
36 Skater Michelle
37 Beatles chart-topper of '64
38 Lily Tomlin's job as Ernestine
39 Japanese cabbage?
40 Alphabet quintet
41 Chest muscle
45 Former U.S. terr.
46 Toadies
48 Whenever you want
49 Aroused
50 Comes after
52 Washstand accessories
54 Catcher's position
57 Cartoonist Silverstein
58 "I thought we ___ deal!"
59 Class of submarines
60 Place to place an ante

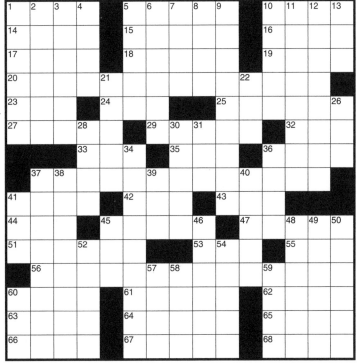

ANSWER, PAGE 95

69

COLLATERAL DAMAGE

ACROSS

1 Pt. of AAA
5 Wordless puzzle
10 Switch on a radio
14 ___ Alto, California
15 Exchange high-fives, e.g.
16 "If I ___ a rich girl" (Gwen Stefani line)
17 Que. or Ont., e.g.
18 Heffalump's creator
19 Neck of the woods
20 Overdue arrest?
22 Rapper who acted in "New Jack City"
23 Put in chains
24 Like one's own language
26 Lyricist Gershwin
27 Food fish
29 Grazing ground
30 Drove over the limit
33 Neighborhood warning?
36 Fork features
38 What golfers try to break
39 Billiards shot
40 Pull a choir member?
43 Manipulative one
44 Alas, in Augsburg
45 Suave to a fault
46 Trucker's ride
48 China shop purchase
50 Chessmen that move diagonally
54 Marine bird
55 Lofty visionary?
58 Scandal suffix
59 Sweet'N Low rival
60 Hit on the noggin
61 Couple, to a gossip columnist
62 Word after Ballet or Charlotte
63 Given the ax, with "off"
64 Turn over
65 Stuffs to the gills
66 Brings to a close

DOWN

1 McIntosh or Granny Smith, e.g.
2 See-through wrap brand
3 Casino machines, briefly
4 Innovative notion
5 Dismissal, as from an office
6 Send to Siberia
7 Wall Street optimist
8 Bone below the elbow
9 Related to the chest
10 Look forward to
11 Lacking compassion
12 Poetry with no set meter
13 Tyrannosaurus rex, for one
21 Vehicle at a drive-in movie
25 Sandler of "Anger Management"
27 Like snakeskin
28 Stag
30 Part of SAC
31 Per item compensation
32 "Some ___ Evening" ("South Pacific" song)
34 Iridescent stone
35 Causing giggles
37 Fruit for flavoring gin
41 Sets of sibling setters, e.g.
42 Baltimore nine
47 Neighbor of Leb.
49 Terse summons
50 Having a ho-hum attitude
51 Continent separator
52 Cross-barred pattern
53 Gives a thrill to
56 Greenish-blue hue
57 The hots

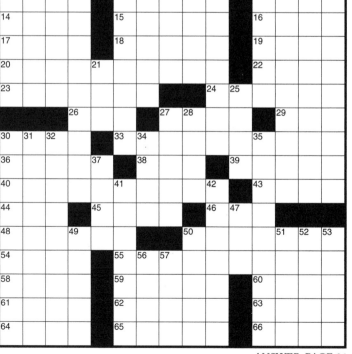

ANSWER, PAGE 96

MYSELF AND I

ACROSS

1 With 67-Across, another title for this puzzle
6 Chemical warfare protection
13 Drop by for a visit
14 Singer nicknamed "The Velvet Fog"
15 Actress Lombard
16 Service volunteer
17 All the time
18 Part of MLK
20 Aykroyd of "The Blues Brothers"
21 Opener for two tins?
22 Lip attachment?
23 Start of many a limerick
25 Jazz pianist Hines, to fans
27 Anesthetized
30 Super serves
31 Hair nets
33 St. Louis footballer
34 Wrongful act
35 Upside-down pendulum
38 Señor's "Sure thing!"
41 The NRC replaced it
42 Cutting the center from
46 Face defacer
47 Nobel physicist Niels
49 Davis of "Do the Right Thing"
50 Lustful looks
52 Funny Foxx
54 Nickelodeon Chihuahua
55 Suffix with lemon
56 It needs oxygen
59 Lacking locks
60 Without rhyme or reason
62 Word to the photographer
64 Interim
65 Radio talk show participant
66 Fill to the brim
67 See 1-Across

DOWN

1 Fellini, for one
2 Home of the Blue Jays
3 Theater light
4 1,000 G's
5 Hostile party
6 Polite fellow
7 "... for ___ care!"
8 Tour of duty
9 Nov. and Dec., e.g.
10 Forte of Erté
11 Nasty politico
12 Most acute
13 Wolfs (down)
14 Antiseptic brand
19 Raggedy doll
22 One-named Nigerian singer
24 They feel animus
26 More comfy
28 "You da ___!"
29 VIP at MIT, e.g.
32 Wild guess
36 Monogrammatic car
37 Frame of mind
38 Peaceful greetings
39 Brewed drink for teetotalers
40 Make fun of
43 Tel Aviv native
44 Big name in ratings
45 Masculine, for example
48 Secessionist soldier
51 He gives gifts in stockings
53 Patsy Cline's record label
57 Wield a blue pencil
58 Baths of Caracalla site
59 Horror icon Lugosi
61 It's dotted
63 Witchy woman

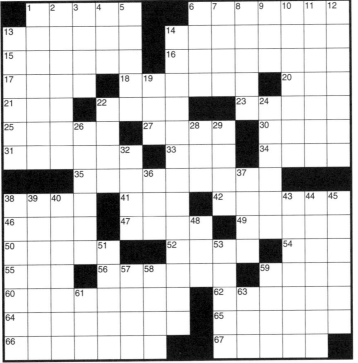

ANSWER, PAGE 81

SUBTLE HINT

ACROSS

1 Get an ___ effort
5 Can't stomach
10 Pay heed
14 Singer Turner
15 Thin pancake
16 Crime-solving game
17 Satyr's stare
18 Hamlet and Ophelia, e.g.
19 Mine and thine
20 Saver of nine, in a saying
23 Mick or Keith
24 ___ school
25 Child's "tattoo," for one
28 Trumpet blast
30 GI mail drop
32 "Huzzah, José!"
33 South American tuber
34 Bolted down

35 Collard greens, e.g.
36 Characteristic of a Type A
40 Lead singer of U2
41 "Cogito, ergo ___"
42 Unmannerly man
43 Mount Rushmore prez
44 Vegas venture
45 Guilty, for example
49 Make it
51 Thar-blows link
53 Anouk of "Lola"
54 One-hit wonder, e.g.
57 Grey of "Cabaret"
59 Slowly, to Salieri
60 Broken bone protector

61 Ancient Andean
62 Pilgrim John
63 Nautical adverb
64 Clothing consumer
65 Emulate a flying squirrel
66 Demond's costar, on '70s TV

DOWN

1 After some delay
2 Ford model
3 Truck weight
4 Chompin' at the bit
5 Band from Sydney
6 Hindu supreme being
7 Skater Sonja
8 Slot for a makeup game

9 Silence in the choir room
10 Christmas carol start
11 Cop
12 Pt. of EEC
13 Twenty questions answer
21 Do a professor's job
22 Wedding words
26 TV lawyer McBeal
27 "Summer of Sam" director Spike
29 Salary increase
31 English coppers
34 PIN requester
35 Wee one's wheels
36 Freddie the Freeloader, e.g.

37 For practical purposes
38 Summary container, figuratively
39 Mother of Isaac
40 Baseball base
44 Front end cover on a car
45 Having air holes
46 Run through
47 Came to an end
48 Lodged under canvas
50 Islam's deity
52 Indian language
55 Refinery refuse
56 Word after dial or earth
57 Carrey of "Bruce Almighty"
58 Plastic ___ Band

ANSWER, PAGE 82

GRAVEYARD SHIFT

ACROSS

1 Some draw them to decide
5 "Green ___ and Ham" (Dr. Seuss classic)
9 Run hot and cold
14 Sandy-colored
15 River to the Caspian
16 Put on cloud nine
17 Expensive meat juice?
19 Earth, in sci-fi
20 Florida seaport
21 High-pitched protests
23 Word before out, in the infield
24 Theoretically
26 In one's salad days
28 Roomy ride
30 Where tires are changed in seconds

33 ATF agents
36 Light music composer Novello
38 "___ you very much!"
39 Country est. in 1948
40 "Ahab the Arab" singer Ray
42 Aachen article
43 Effective input
45 Miami-___ County
46 Bring in
47 Come to light
49 Steer clear of
51 Give the nod to
53 Asian lake
57 Ministerial nickname
59 "Fried Green Tomatoes ..." author Fannie

61 Frequent word in mastheads
62 Sun Valley locale
64 Pull actor Brooks across the floor?
66 Backus voice role
67 Enya's homeland
68 Designer Saab
69 Change, as a manuscript
70 Seeing trouble
71 Leave unchanged

DOWN

1 Resulted in
2 Neptune's realm
3 Freddie the Freeloader, e.g.
4 Go beyond
5 Continent of Ger.
6 Anatomy author carried on?

7 Collapsed under pressure
8 In a furtive fashion
9 Divers' wear
10 Brown beverage
11 Change the steepness?
12 Versailles verb
13 Bring up, as children
18 Open wide
22 "___ Goes the Weasel"
25 Strike from a script, say
27 Last in a series
29 Exploding suns
31 Ready to go into the service
32 Venus Flytrap's radio station
33 Closed hand
34 Birthright seller of the Bible

35 Teetotaler's havoc?
37 Bloody whim?
40 Turnip greens, cornbread, and such
41 ___ beer
44 NBC sketch show
46 Goes through again
48 D.C. figure
50 Floppy disk contents
52 Walks through water
54 Refine, as ore
55 Causing chill bumps
56 To this point
57 Winter coating
58 Cheese with a coating made of wax
60 Sandpaper coating
63 Pet name
65 "Man!"

ANSWER, PAGE 85

FILL MY CUP

ACROSS

1 Legacy from mom or dad
6 Sale words
10 Briquette
14 Words said with a shrug
16 University of Hawaii's backfield in motion?
17 Facial foundation
18 Mayberry elbow-bender
19 Hosp. sites
20 Subdivision maps
21 "Bad, Bad Leroy Brown" singer Jim
22 Modeling material
23 Shoe without a lace
24 Uses worms, in a way
27 Police officer's badge
29 Diarist Nin
30 Gridiron three-pointer
33 Baby bottom soother
34 Tie the knot
35 "Class Reunion" author Jaffe
36 Loser at the craps table
38 Hardly sophisticated
39 Like cheddar in a grilled cheese
40 Dirty rats
41 Beef cuts
43 Lend a hand
44 Wound up
45 '70s Freddie Prinze role
47 "Just as I thought!"
50 European front?
51 Throat medication
53 Stead
54 Acting in front of a live audience
55 ACC athlete
56 First Lady after Eleanor
57 Ran without moving

DOWN

1 Lionel alternative
2 Have a good laugh
3 Black-and-white divers
4 "Now ___ seen everything!"
5 Forehead sides
6 Astronaut's "thumbs-up": Var.
7 Leave alone, to an editor
8 Don of talk radio
9 IRA for small companies
10 Glee club, e.g.
11 In the open
12 Wonderland visitor
13 ___ printer
15 The Oscars and others
21 Like some dorms
22 Broth "for the soul," in motivational books
23 Easter flower
24 Domino of the ivories
25 Instant starter?
26 Amphibian without scales
27 Was the father of
28 Word on a towel
30 "Mommie Dearest" star Dunaway
31 Vampire novelist Rice
32 Produces eggs
34 "Miracle" nine of '69
37 Sommer of "A Shot in the Dark"
38 Easter Island statues, e.g.
40 La ___ League
41 Support for a clown
42 "Thin Ice" actress Sonja
43 Mountaintop experiences
45 Orange road marker
46 "Gilligan's Island" housing
47 Asia's ___ Sea
48 Elephantine
49 Parodied
51 Ear interior
52 From Jan. 1 to now

ANSWER, PAGE 86

CONFLICT OF INTEREST

ACROSS

1 Like some ears or elbows
5 Hindu religious teacher
10 Abdul-Jabbar's alma mater
14 "Song of the South" syllables after "Zip"
15 Wrinkle-resistant synthetic
16 "Iliad" city
17 Psyche divisions
18 Biggest part
20 Apartment?
22 River of Tiny Tim's town
23 Heads up
24 "East of Eden" son
25 Plays kneesies, for example
27 Group of do-nothings?
31 Sponsorship
32 Rival of Helena and Max

33 Yokohama "yes"
34 Madeline of "Blazing Saddles"
35 Surrealist Max
36 A natural, for one
37 Attendance fig., often
38 Tee off
39 Not as many
40 Take umbrage at something?
42 Dwindles, with "out"
43 Notion, in Nice
44 "___ is human ..."
45 User of an old phone
48 Need for five axles?
51 Way to a highway, perhaps

53 ___ Bora (Afghan region)
54 Mark of omission
55 Lavatory sign
56 Seemingly forever
57 Nonlethal phaser setting
58 Home run, or home fries source
59 Hook's henchman

DOWN

1 Jethro Bodine portrayer Max
2 Cutting part
3 They're bright on Broadway
4 Give Brockovich an exam?
5 One side in eightball

6 Formal orders
7 Skin cream additive
8 Montego Bay male
9 Stylish way?
10 Dag Hammarskjöld's successor
11 Crack the books at the eleventh hour
12 Anecdotal knowledge
13 Assents on the sea
19 Land on the sea
21 College entrance exams
24 On pins and needles
25 One who plays possum, for example
26 Take for a while

27 Comeback in a kids' argument
28 Bathing place
29 What "-vore" means
30 Wedding cake features
32 Banks or Bilko
35 "Door's open, have a seat"?
36 Cyberspace ceremonies?
38 Peaks in Peru
39 Dozens of inches
41 Actress Brennan
42 Give thought to
44 Poke fun at
45 Family men
46 Big name in rap
47 Darrow's org.
48 Track advisor
49 Ocean flier
50 Ed.'s request
52 Part of a gene's makeup

ANSWER, PAGE 89

NAPOLEON BLOWN-APART

ACROSS

1 Compadre of Porthos
6 Eban of Israel
10 Do a slow burn
14 Tuscan city
15 Race in a regatta
16 Driver's license datum
17 Longtime South Carolina senator Thurmond
18 Event with a king and queen
19 Similar in nature
20 "Is lunch ready?" e.g.?
22 "The Lonely Bull" trumpeter Herb
24 Flair
25 Highbrow
26 "It's My Party" singer Gore
29 Long-jump foul?
32 Seawater tint
33 Golf pro's concern
35 Lookout point
36 We sit on them
38 Since 1/1, on a bank stmt.
39 Practices punching
41 Partner of vigor
42 Town of an animal-friendly saint
45 Old U.S. gas brand
46 King Kong attacking Chaney?
48 Like the Titanic
50 Boca ___, Florida
51 Slammin' Sammy
52 Eat sparingly
54 Borrowed cornbread?
58 Series terminal
59 Ring-tailed critter
61 Con game
62 Frosty covering
63 Graceland middle name
64 Prefix with line or mine
65 Cosby-Culp series
66 Trust, with "on"
67 Sat to be shot

DOWN

1 Pt. of PTA
2 Former Yugoslav head
3 Lifesaver
4 Where twins may sit?
5 Store freebie
6 Colorado ski spot
7 Vamp Theda
8 Short profile
9 Annual publication
10 Fasten with a pop
11 Censure
12 Commander, in Arab
13 Took place, with "on"
21 Sets down
23 Strides easily
25 Dispatches
26 Grub that most people won't eat
27 Fit out
28 Place for hiking, boating, and such
29 Language that may be Vulgar?
30 Vikings, e.g.
31 Bean on the screen
34 Perdue rival
37 Comet's guider
40 Yoko in jail?
43 Model of a fast one
44 Words after "the heat"
47 Annie who got her gun on the stage
49 Exhausted
51 Cher's hubby, once
52 Roz portrayer on "Frasier"
53 "Really?"
54 Office wagering
55 Racetrack info
56 Onetime Met Tommie
57 Unhip type
60 Salem's st.

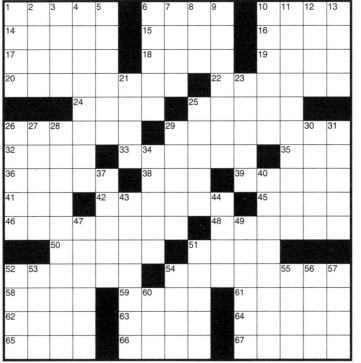

ANSWER, PAGE 90

I ONLY HAVE I'S FOR YOU

ACROSS

1 Hungarian composer Franz
6 X, on a greeting card
10 California's ___ Valley
14 "He's Got the Whole World ___ Hands"
15 Colored eye part
16 Work with needles
17 Hairpieces for clowns
19 Former Spanish enclave in Morocco
20 Waitperson's reward
21 "If only that were true!"
22 Barbeque accessories
23 Alternative nickname to Pat
24 Hearty swallows
25 Runs off, in a way
28 Fresh Prince Will
29 Help for the stumped
30 Electrify
33 Sets for couch potatoes
36 Performed, per Shakespeare
38 "___ for Innocent" (Sue Grafton novel)
39 XXI tripled
41 Fed. support benefit
42 Take the chance
45 Where the U.S. Senate meets
46 Peevish states
48 Martina of tennis
50 Work period
51 "Of Thee ___"
53 Russian pancakes
54 Mixes up
55 Basinger of "8 Mile"
58 Navel buildup
59 Underwater sport
61 Need a scratch
62 Common UFO shape
63 Curtain material
64 Attention-getters: Var.
65 Egyptian fertility goddess
66 "T-R-O-U-B-L-E" singer Travis

DOWN

1 English elevator
2 Cross inscription
3 Model in a bottle
4 Change course
5 Souvenir shop item
6 Fuzzy fruits
7 Word before stew or whiskey
8 Resigned respiration
9 Puncture sound
10 "Never mind!"
11 Conflict among family members, e.g.
12 Restaurant freebies
13 Suffix with tonsil
18 Peel in a drink
22 Supper in a sty
23 Blowup causes
24 Ascending sizes, briefly
25 High degrees
26 Jacob who chronicled slum life
27 Not clearly marked
28 "You bet!" in Yucatán
31 Unhappy fan's reaction
32 Smits of the NBA
34 One of a Caesarean trio
35 Canine attack commands
37 Lopez of pop
40 Place to walk, for short
43 Electronics co.
44 Show horse?
47 Last innings
49 Be firm
50 Narrow cuts
51 Identification phrase, or another title for this puzzle
52 Makes, as a putt
53 Radar screen flash
54 Dashes through the snow
55 Opera's ___ Te Kanawa
56 Pt. of a monogram
57 Those running the place: Abbr.
59 Cold war abbr.
60 Home film player

ANSWER, PAGE 93

THEMELESS CHALLENGER

ACROSS
1 High country
6 Boom
10 Hospital count
14 Musical treasure
15 Loved by the camera
17 Rather, slangily
18 Sign, as an agreement
19 Potato, for one
20 Triumphs academically
21 Hellenic vowel
22 Looks up to
24 Southern constellation
26 Feel poorly
27 "In the Heat of the Night" city
32 "Phirst-rate"

33 Crane site
35 Blue toon
36 Jet type
37 Milo of "Ulysses"
39 Nicky, in "Funny Girl"
40 Some seafood lovers
42 Summer colors
43 From the start, after "de"
44 Dido's love
46 USPS round
47 Hurdle for some coll. students
48 Calendar rarity
51 A-Rod's org.
53 Trapped
57 Say "cap'n," say
59 Regular burner
60 ___ wind

61 To and fro, for example
62 "Mother Night" star
63 Trueheart of the comics
64 Crew equipment
65 Day one

DOWN
1 Refinement
2 "See ya"
3 Girl in a Beach Boys song title
4 Major addition
5 Top with jewels
6 Most like a sauna
7 Lead reducer
8 Metamorphose

9 Candy wrapper word
10 "Ever so humble" introduction
11 Non-PC suffix
12 Morse taps
13 Inverness inhabitant, e.g.
16 Understands
23 Paul of "Little Miss Sunshine"
25 "... poem lovely as ___"
28 In with
29 Grapevines, sometimes
30 Itinerary item
31 Big do
32 Response to a charge

34 It isn't waisted
38 Whaling, e.g.
41 Drawing rooms
45 Brazilian musician Mendes
49 "West Side Story" woman
50 Question variety
52 Tours topper
53 Gershwin title start
54 Mane location
55 Hieroglyphic snakes
56 Co. leaders
58 Canadian coin flier

ANSWER, PAGE 94

78

7 INFLAMMATORY ENDING

```
P O M P   C A R T   M A T Z O
O N U S   A V E R   C O H E N
U C L A   S A S E   K R A U T
T E L L I T L I K E I T I S
    M O R A N   R N A
L E T I N O N   P I L S N E R
O T I S   C R O C E   O L A
T H A T S T H E W A Y I T I S
S I R   T R E N D   N E A P
A C A C I A S   E M B A S S Y
    A N I   T R O O P
  Y O U K N O W H O W I T I S
D E N S E   L I O N   N A T O
E L M E R   I N R I   C L I P
B L E S S   N E N E   H E S S
```

25 A DOZEN RABBIT FEET

```
R I C A   A R A B S   P U T T
E L H I   T E N E T   A B B A
S L A M   M A K E A   T O I L
T U N E R   M A R C H H A R E
E M C E E D   B Y O   T D S
D I E   D I S C O   P A S S E
U N I T   S H U T S I N
P E T E R C O T T O N T A I L
    R E S P E L L   E L M O
H U M P H   W R E A K   L I V
U S A   A R I   R E B A T E
B U G S B U N N Y   G A L A S
E R G O   I D I O M   T O T E
R E I N   N O T R E   O N E A
T R E S   S W E E T   N E S T
```

43 STICK TO CARROT STICKS

```
O C H S   A D L I B   S I G H
L O A M   I R O N Y   A T R A
D I V E   D E C O R   P E O N
P L E A S E D O N O T   R U G
R E T R O     T E A A C T
O D O   B O P   F E E D T H E
    P I L A T E   A E O N
    V E G E T A R I A N S
B O O R   H O N C H O
A N I M A L S   S C I   P A C
H E C A T E     K N O L L
A N E   T O T H E P E O P L E
M O B S   N O U S E   S A D E
A T O P   I N L A W   E R A S
S E X Y   D E L I S   S T Y E
```

61 MOTH MENU

```
A L E C   A R L E N   C B E R
P O L O   S E E N O   O L G A
O A H U   S T E I N   M O O G
  D I N N E R J A C K E T S
    T A R O   C O I F
A S C E N T     M A I L E R
L A H R   S I L O S   R A T A
E M O T E   M A N   P S Y C H
    P O R K P I E H A T S
A D S   N O R T H E R   E L F
N A T   E S O   A R A   Y E R
A M I S S   V O N   D I E G O
C O C K T A I L D R E S S E S
I N K Y   I S L E T   M O N T
N E S S   R E A D E   E N D S
```

8 FINDING NEMO

S	P	E	D		H	I	T	O	N		C	R	A	T
L	A	M	E		A	R	E	N	A		R	O	S	H
O	N	E	M	O	M	E	N	T	P	L	E	A	S	E
	C	R	U	X		D	O	H		A	T	R	E	E
Z	A	G	R	E	B		R	E	S	T	E	A	S	Y
I	K	E		N	I	T		H	I	E		T	S	E
P	E	N	N		B	O	L	O	G	N	A			
	S	T	O	N	E	M	O	U	N	T	A	I	N	
		R	E	L	A	P	S	E		A	M	I	D	
A	R	A		G	O	T		E	T	S		P	G	A
D	I	C	T	A	T	O	R		S	T	J	O	H	N
O	C	T	E	T		S	O	S		O	U	S	T	
P	H	O	N	E	M	O	U	T	H	P	I	E	C	E
T	I	N	T		A	U	G	U	R		C	R	A	G
S	E	E	S		O	P	E	N	S		E	S	P	O

26 SHAKESPEARE FROM THE REAR

A	S	T	I		D	O	L	E	S		A	P	E	D
T	O	E	S		O	P	A	R	T		M	O	V	E
C	R	A	M	A	N	T	O	N	Y		O	L	E	O
O	E	R		B	E	E	S			S	C	A	N	
S	L	U	R	R	E	D		A	M	O	O	R	O	F
T	Y	P	E	O		V	I	A	L		C	D	T	
			S	A	L	I	E	R	I		L	A	D	D
	O	U	T	D	A	M	N	E	D	T	O	P	S	
E	P	P	S		L	E	A	D	S	I	N			
S	E	P		B	A	A	L			P	E	C	O	S
O	N	E	S	O	W	N		C	H	O	R	A	L	E
	F	R	A	Y		G	O	O	F		R	I	N	
M	I	C	K		B	A	R	D	O	F	N	O	V	A
T	R	U	E		U	R	I	A	H		I	L	E	T
V	E	T	S		M	E	N	S	A		P	E	R	E

44 CYBER-CHUCKLE

H	A	L	F		P	E	A	K		P	A	U	L	A
E	L	I	E		A	X	L	E		R	I	S	E	R
A	T	M	E		R	U	L	E		I	M	E	A	N
L	O	B	L	O	L	L	Y	P	I	N	E			
		S	P	O	T		U	T	T	E	R	S		
S	I	M	M	E	R	S		P	T	A		E	N	O
I	D	E	A	L	S		G	O	O	D	S	H	I	P
D	I	L	L		G	O	N			H	I	D	E	
L	O	L	L	I	P	O	P		L	A	U	R	E	N
E	T	O		N	E	E		W	A	L	T	E	R	S
	S	W	E	A	R	S		A	B	E	T			
		P	H	I	L	O	L	O	G	I	S	T	S	
E	L	S	I	E		O	D	E	R		G	L	E	E
T	O	S	C	A		N	O	S	E		H	U	R	L
C	L	A	S	P		G	R	A	D		T	G	I	F

62 GEOMETRIC RELATIONSHIPS

T	O	S	S		B	E	B	O	P		S	P	A	S
U	P	T	O		I	N	U	R	E		A	O	N	E
C	A	R	L		D	O	S	E	S		M	U	T	T
S	Q	U	A	R	E	S	H	O	O	T	E	R		
O	U	N	C	E	S				S	H	I	R	E	
N	E	G	E	V		S	A	L	T	P	E	T	E	R
			E	M	P	L	O	Y		R	O	A	R	
C	I	R	C	L	E	O	F	F	R	I	E	N	D	S
O	L	E	O		T	R	I	T	E	R				
D	E	C	O	R	A	T	E	S		W	I	S	E	R
S	T	A	K	E				F	I	N	A	L	E	
	L	O	V	E	T	R	I	A	N	G	L	E	S	
A	C	L	U		G	R	A	N	D		M	O	V	E
P	O	E	T		G	I	J	O	E		A	M	E	N
E	N	D	S		S	P	A	N	S		R	E	N	T

17 MICKEY MOUSE BREAKS DOWN

```
N O T A B I T   R O A D I E S
A V A R I C E   E N C O R E S
T A P E D E C K L E T T E R S
      T D S   R I I S
C A C H E   G A E L   A H E M
I S L A N D O F F L O R I D A
A T O     O P T S   F A B I O
  A C R I D     A T B A T
L I K E D   N C A R   C I O
C R I M I N A L S M E T H O D
D E N Y   E T A L   R H I N E
      H E I R   A R I
T A K E A D V A N T A G E O F
E P I S T L E   R O T H I R A
N E M E S E S   A M A S S E D
```

35 PEN PALS

```
B I G B A N G   S T O R E U P
A R O U S A L   N O T O N C E
L A R G E M O T O R C Y C L E
K E Y S   W I R E     S A L
      O S E   B E A M E
C H A U V I N I S T I C G U Y
H Y S T E R I A   G O A P E
A D S   L E X   D O H   Y O N
I R E S T   S E N T I E N T
R O T T E N S C O U N D R E L
    P R I M A   S T E
N U T   P E R M   A F A R
A R K A N S A S A T H L E T E
S L O T C A R   M A I L M A N
A S S E R T S   A R M Y A N T
```

53 IN THE SHORT RUN

```
M O N K   N A C L   A N I S E
I C O N   E C H O   D A N T E
D A M E   W H A T D O T H E Y
D R I E S T   O T I S   A P O
L I N D A   S T A G E   S S R
E N A   L I L I   A T O E
C A L L A R A C E O F M E N
    I M A N   B R E A
  H A V I N G L E S S H A I R
B O N E     E R O S   S P A
R E G   E P C O T   E A T A T
I C E   L E A P   A S L A N T
B A L D E R D A S H   T I E R
E K I N G   G R A M   E R M A
D E C A Y   E D G E   R E A P
```

71 MYSELF AND I

```
  I T S M E   G A S M A S K
S T O P I N   M E L T O R M E
C A R O L E   E N L I S T E E
A L O T   M A R T I N   D A N
R I N   S Y N C     T H E R E
F A T H A   N U M B   A C E S
S N O O D S   R A M   T O R T
      M E T R O N O M E
S I S I   A E C   C O R I N G
A C N E   B O H R   O S S I E
L E E R S   R E D D   R E N
A D E   A E R O B E   B A L D
A T R A N D O M   C H E E S E
M E A N T I M E   C A L L E R
S A T I A T E   A G A I N
```

18 A HATFIELD WHO WAS THE REAL MCCOY

U	S	S	R		A	T	L	A	S		O	R	E	S
M	I	T	E		M	A	U	D	E		T	O	R	A
B	L	U	E	P	E	N	C	I	L		T	O	R	I
R	O	C	K	A	N	D	R	O	L	L		S	O	N
A	S	K	E	D		Y	E	S		E	V	E	N	T
			D	R	S				H	E	A	V	E	N
B	B	C		E	N	C	O	R	E		L	E	O	I
R	O	O		S	O	U	L	A	N	D		L	U	C
I	N	N	S		W	E	D	G	I	E		T	S	K
M	E	D	L	E	Y				E	L	S			
S	T	E	A	L		A	U	D		T	I	F	F	S
T	I	N		I	N	S	P	I	R	A	T	I	O	N
O	R	S	O		O	P	E	R	A	S	C	O	R	E
N	E	E	R		T	E	N	E	T		O	N	E	A
E	D	D	Y		A	N	D	R	E		M	A	S	K

36 POOL PARTY

R	E	P	S		A	D	O	B	E		A	T	I	P
A	P	E	D		R	E	B	U	T		C	A	N	I
W	A	D	I	N	G	B	I	R	D		R	I	P	E
D	U	D		O	U	S	T	S		M	E	L	E	E
A	L	L	U	D	E			A	M	A		F	A	Y
T	E	E	N	S		D	I	R	T	Y	R	I	C	E
A	T	R	A		S	E	C		W	E	A	N	E	D
			G	E	N	E	A	U	T	R	Y			
S	L	E	E	V	E		R	A	F		G	A	P	S
C	A	R	D	E	A	L	E	R		M	U	S	I	C
A	V	E		R	D	A			C	A	N	A	R	Y
R	E	M	I	T		G	O	F	A	R		R	A	T
E	R	I	C		M	O	T	O	R	M	O	U	T	H
U	N	T	O		G	O	T	U	P		F	L	E	E
P	E	E	N		S	N	O	R	E		F	E	D	S

54 COMPARATIVELY SPEAKING

S	A	H	I	B		S	H	O	T	S		H	O	S	T
O	L	I	V	E		T	A	G	U	P		I	T	H	E
A	L	L	E	R	G	I	C	R	E	A	C	T	I	O	N
N	F	L		R	I	L	K	E		R	U	M	O	R	S
D	O	S		A	S	T	I		C	E	L	E	S	T	E
S	U	I	T			S	T	E	E	R		N	E	S	S
O	R	D	A	I	N			G	R	I	P				
	S	E	R	V	I	N	G	O	F	B	A	C	O	N	
			Y	G	O	R			S	N	A	P	A	T	
C	A	T	V		H	E	R	B	S		D	E	M	O	
O	R	I	E	N	T	S		A	T	O	M		N	E	T
M	I	N	N	O	W		V	I	O	L	A		D	D	T
M	O	S	T	D	E	V	I	L	M	A	Y	C	A	R	E
I	S	E	E		A	E	S	O	P		A	S	T	O	R
T	O	L	D		R	E	A	R	S		S	T	E	P	S

72 SUBTLE HINT

A	F	O	R		A	B	H	O	R		O	B	E	Y
T	I	N	A		C	R	E	P	E		C	L	U	E
L	E	E	R		D	A	N	E	S		O	U	R	S
A	S	T	I	T	C	H	I	N	T	I	M	E		
S	T	O	N	E		M	E	D		D	E	C	A	L
T	A	N	T	A	R	A		A	P	O		O	L	E
			O	C	A		A	T	E		K	A	L	E
	H	I	G	H	I	N	T	E	N	S	I	T	Y	
B	O	N	O		S	U	M		C	A	D			
A	B	E		B	E	T		V	E	R	D	I	C	T
G	O	F	A	R		S	H	E		A	I	M	E	E
	F	L	A	S	H	I	N	T	H	E	P	A	N	
J	O	E	L		L	E	N	T	O		C	A	S	T
I	N	C	A		A	L	D	E	N		A	L	E	E
M	O	T	H		G	L	I	D	E		R	E	D	D

9 CO-PILOTS

```
HOGWILD ALAMODE
OCEANIA MARINER
PHANTOMJETFLIER
SSR ONSALE ENDS
    VWS MIRE
HEMI YEA GASH
ERASURES BERLIN
LIGHTINTHESTOVE
PENNED AUNTIEEM
 SAUR BYE ESSO
   OEIL MIR
ILSA LOOPED HUG
SITCOMPROTOTYPE
BEATLES SOLOMON
NURSERY HOSANNA
```

27 WAY TO GOH!

```
TAXI NITRO AGOG
ABED OCHER LIVE
DINO TAUNT IVAN
STANDINGOH BELT
   TAFT ONIT
CATCHY TIDE HMS
ASEA COCOABEAN
SPARENOHEXPENSE
TIMELIMIT NOSE
ENS AGES BIDDER
  PENH SODA
GLIB TAEKWANDOH
RARE OLLIE EIRE
EMIR WEBER ACED
WATT LEERY RELY
```

45 HUNGER FOR KNOWLEDGE

```
CAFE MOBS OHARA
URAL ALOE PANIC
BERM ALLTHERAGE
ITOOKMATHAND
CHURN LICKED
ATEITUPSONOWMY
  TENET GRAIN
JAMB AGEOF EIRE
ELIOT EVIAN
TEETHARECOATED
TENSER ROLEO
 WITHCALCULUS
PAYASYOUGO PICT
EVENT CREW EEEE
PAPAS KLEE ESSO
```

63 ARTIFICIAL GREENERY

```
ATME AMEN HULAS
FEELSMALL ELATE
BATMOBILE ANDRE
 SHOULDERBLADES
AHA LEE ASSIST
BONO SNIPS ETO
SPORT NEATO
 LEAVESALONE
  OXIDE PEGGY
ESS EATAT IGLU
ACTNOW ORB WIL
SHOOTSSTRAIGHT
TOWIT LATINRITE
LOIRE UPANDATEM
ALTER GEES BERT
```

10 WHATSA MATTER?

```
C A S K   E M B E R   S O S A
H I K E   V A L L I   P R E T
E R I N   I C O M E   R E A L
A P T   S C H O O L B E L L A
P I T A S T O P S   Y E S E S
E L I D E       D E S E R T
N O S E   G R A D E A
  T H E G O O D E A R T H A
    R A N O F F   H O L M
A M O R A L     T A M P A
T E N E T   M E N S A W E A R
M A L T A L I Q U O R   S C I
O N I T   A T U R N   S P I N
S I N O   I T I S I   T U N A
T E E N   T Y P E A   E N O S
```

28 STAR-CROSSED

```
S L A V   T V S E T   S M U G
T O R A   H I K E R   H A N D
I R A N   I S E E A   I N C A
R E B E C C A D E M O R N A Y
    S A K S     S L A P
L A S S I E   L E A S E
O C E A N   R O D T A Y L O R
A N E W   B O R G E   M I R E
D E M I M O O R E   P A R E E
    L E Y T E   B A C A L L
  S I L T     S O I L
C H R I S T I A N S L A T E R
I O W A   A N V I L   I O N A
T R I M   T R I P E   N O O K
Y E N S   S I S S Y   E L L E
```

46 THE BODY POLITIC

```
A R C H   R O B B   A C I D S
T O R I   I N R E   B O N E T
H O U S E S E A T   R A S T A
E T E   L E D G E   A C T E R
A F L O A T   G L A D H A N D
R O L L T O P   S E E N T O
T R A D E   F E L T   S T E M
      R E C R O O M
N A S T   P S S T   A N D I E
E N C A S E   S O L O I N G
W A R C H E S T   R A T E D G
S T O K E   T R E A D   T I E
M O O L A   P A R T Y H E A D
A L G E R   A M M O   E R N O
N E E D S   T S A R   A S S N
```

64 WHERE OFF

```
H A R E   G I F T S   C A T S
O D E S   A D I E U   L I R E
L A T S   R E N A L   A R I A
B Y Y O U R S E L F   S T E W
E A P   Z E T A   U P S I D E
I G E T I T   R A R A   M O E
N O S E     A T W I T S E N D
    E N O S   E C H O
I N A N Y C A S E   W H E E
M O N   P E P E   C A N A R Y
A M A N D A   C A A N   N N E
G I G I   N E A R M I S S E S
I N R E   A R N I E   P O S H
N E A L   U T T E R   A L T O
G E M S   T E S L A   M O O T
```

19 TIGHTEN YOUR BELT

P	E	S	C	I		B	L	O	B		R	E	P	S
E	L	T	O	N		L	I	M	E		O	R	L	Y
P	L	A	N	A		A	N	N	A		B	R	A	N
		C	H	A	S	T	I	T	Y	B	O	N	O	
B	E	H	O	O	V	E			N	A	I	L	E	D
O	R	A	C	L	E		C	H	I	L	E			
G	A	R	T	E	R	S	N	A	K	E		S	S	E
U	S	E	S			A	O	L			P	A	I	L
S	E	M		C	O	T	T	O	N	C	A	N	D	Y
		D	O	N	E	E		E	A	S	E	L	S	
E	M	B	E	R	S			O	A	K	T	R	E	E
B	I	B	L	E	T	H	U	M	P	E	R			
S	L	A	T		A	O	N	E		P	A	P	E	R
E	L	L	A		G	R	I	N		A	M	I	G	O
N	I	L	S		E	A	T	S		N	I	X	O	N

37 ENOUGH!

M	E	S	H		B	G	I	R	L		A	P	E	S
E	L	I	E		R	O	S	I	E		R	A	V	E
A	N	N	S		A	D	O	P	T		I	L	I	E
D	I	G	S	I	N	O	N	E	S	H	E	E	L	S
O	N	T		M	D	T			G	O	L	F	E	R
W	O	O	D	E	N		A	T	O	P		A	Y	E
			A	T	E	A	S	E		A	C	E	D	
		D	R	A	W	T	H	E	L	I	N	E		
A	G	I	N		R	E	M	A	R	K				
I	R	A		S	P	A	N		W	E	A	V	E	S
R	O	L	L	E	R		C	C	S		O	D	E	
P	U	T	O	N	E	S	F	O	O	T	D	O	W	N
U	P	O	N		S	H	A	M	U		E	D	Y	S
M	I	N	E		T	I	M	E	R		P	O	N	E
P	E	E	R		O	V	E	R	T		P	O	N	D

55 AIRPORT HOTEL

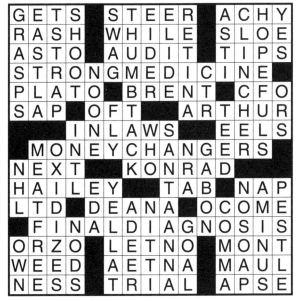

G	E	T	S		S	T	E	E	R		A	C	H	Y
R	A	S	H		W	H	I	L	E		S	L	O	E
A	S	T	O		A	U	D	I	T		T	I	P	S
S	T	R	O	N	G	M	E	D	I	C	I	N	E	
P	L	A	T	O		B	R	E	N	T		C	F	O
S	A	P		O	F	T		A	R	T	H	U	R	
		I	N	L	A	W	S		E	E	L	S		
	M	O	N	E	Y	C	H	A	N	G	E	R	S	
N	E	X	T		K	O	N	R	A	D				
H	A	I	L	E	Y		T	A	B		N	A	P	
L	T	D		D	E	A	N	A		O	C	O	M	E
	F	I	N	A	L	D	I	A	G	N	O	S	I	S
O	R	Z	O		L	E	T	N	O		M	O	N	T
W	E	E	D		A	E	T	N	A		M	A	U	L
N	E	S	S		T	R	I	A	L		A	P	S	E

73 GRAVEYARD SHIFT

L	O	T	S		E	G	G	S		W	A	V	E	R
E	C	R	U		U	R	A	L		E	L	A	T	E
D	E	A	R	G	R	A	V	Y		T	E	R	R	A
T	A	M	P	A		Y	E	L	P	S		Y	E	R
O	N	P	A	P	E	R		Y	O	U	N	G		
			S	E	D	A	N		P	I	T	R	O	W
F	E	D	S		I	V	O	R		T	H	A	N	K
I	S	R		S	T	E	V	E	N	S		D	E	R
S	A	Y	S	O		D	A	D	E		R	E	A	P
T	U	R	N	U	P		E	V	A	D	E			
	A	L	L	O	W		A	R	A	L	S	E	A	
R	E	V		F	L	A	G	G		T	I	M	E	S
I	D	A	H	O		D	R	A	G	A	V	E	R	Y
M	A	G	O	O		E	I	R	E		E	L	I	E
E	M	E	N	D		S	T	Y	E		S	T	E	T

20 HOLY MEN, HOLEY TEETH

G	O	T	I	T		K	I	T	S		S	P	I	T
I	N	A	N	E		I	N	R	E		A	O	N	E
M	E	C	C	A		S	T	O	W		N	O	R	A
M	A	H	A	R	I	S	H	I	S		T	R	E	K
E	L	S		A	C	M	E		M	A	T	T	E	
	S	T	H	E	L	E	N	A		A	R	T		
S	U	P	S		I	N	E	Z		S	E	T		
T	R	A	N	S	C	E	N	D	D	E	N	T	A	L
E	S	S		K	A	L	E		F	E	T	E		
P	A	T		I	M	M	O	R	T	A	L			
A	M	I	S	S		F	A	L	L		A	R	K	
S	I	N	K		M	E	D	I	C	A	T	I	O	N
I	N	G	A		O	N	U	S		S	I	D	L	E
D	O	I	T		B	Y	T	E		K	N	E	L	L
E	R	N	E		S	A	Y	S		A	S	S	E	T

38 MARCHING ORDERS

C	U	B	A	N		A	P	O	P		N	O	O	N
A	G	O	R	A		C	O	L	A		E	N	V	Y
P	L	A	I	T		T	S	A	R		P	E	E	P
P	I	Z	Z	A	H	U	T		A	T	H	A	N	D
			L	E	A		A	L	I	E	N	S		
M	U	L	T	I	P	L	Y	B	Y	T	W	O		
O	H	A	R	E		O	U	Z	O		T	K	O	
L	O	D	E		R	O	U	T	E		S	H	A	G
T	H	Y		N	E	W	S		S	H	E	L	L	
	F	I	D	D	L	E	R	S	T	H	R	E	E	
F	I	N	A	L	S		W	A	Y					
K	I	N	S	K	I		B	A	L	L	F	O	U	R
O	L	G	A		G	R	I	N		E	L	I	Z	A
O	M	E	N		H	E	R	D		R	E	L	I	C
P	Y	R	E		T	A	D	A		S	A	S	S	Y

56 LIE IN WAIT

M	O	O	R		R	A	G	S		T	E	M	P	T
A	R	L	O		I	D	L	E		A	N	O	D	E
R	E	E	L		C	O	O	T		P	O	N	T	E
C	O	O	L	Y	O	U	R	H	E	E	L	S		
		B	A	T	T	Y		G	R	A	T	I	N	
A	S	L	A	N	T		S	A	E		E	N	E	
S	T	I	C	K	A	R	O	U	N	D		R	C	A
T	O	O	K		E	R	R		A	H	O	T		
H	O	N		P	L	A	Y	F	O	R	T	I	M	E
M	P	S		I	A	M		F	A	L	T	E	R	
A	S	S	I	G	N		S	H	A	V	E			
	H	O	L	D	U	P	A	M	I	N	U	T	E	
C	R	A	T	E		Z	U	N	I		G	R	E	Y
C	A	R	A	T		I	N	O	N		T	S	A	R
C	H	E	S	S		S	K	I	D		H	A	R	E

74 FILL MY CUP

T	R	A	I	T		A	S	I	S		C	O	A	L
Y	O	U	V	E	G	O	T	M	E		H	U	L	A
C	A	K	E	M	A	K	E	U	P		O	T	I	S
O	R	S		P	L	A	T	S		C	R	O	C	E
			C	L	A	Y		L	O	A	F	E	R	
F	I	S	H	E	S		S	H	I	E	L	D		
A	N	A	I	S		F	I	E	L	D	G	O	A	L
T	A	L	C		M	A	R	R	Y		R	O	N	A
S	N	A	K	E	E	Y	E	S		C	O	R	N	Y
		M	E	L	T	E	D		L	O	U	S	E	S
S	H	A	N	K	S		H	E	L	P				
T	E	N	S	E		C	H	I	C	O		A	H	A
I	N	D	O		C	O	U	G	H	S	Y	R	U	P
L	I	E	U		O	N	T	H	E	S	T	A	G	E
T	E	R	P		B	E	S	S		I	D	L	E	D

11 HE PLAYED GOD ...

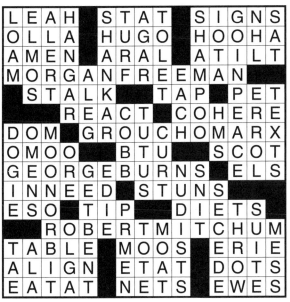

L	E	A	H		S	T	A	T		S	I	G	N	S
O	L	L	A		H	U	G	O		H	O	O	H	A
A	M	E	N		A	R	A	L		A	T	I	L	T
M	O	R	G	A	N	F	R	E	E	M	A	N		
	S	T	A	L	K			T	A	P		P	E	T
	R	E	A	C	T		C	O	H	E	R	E		
D	O	M		G	R	O	U	C	H	O	M	A	R	X
O	M	O	O		B	T	U			S	C	O	T	
G	E	O	R	G	E	B	U	R	N	S		E	L	S
I	N	N	E	E	D		S	T	U	N	S			
E	S	O		T	I	P		D	I	E	T	S		
			R	O	B	E	R	T	M	I	T	C	H	U	M
T	A	B	L	E		M	O	O	S		E	R	I	E
A	L	I	G	N		E	T	A	T		D	O	T	S
E	A	T	A	T		N	E	T	S		E	W	E	S

29 INTIMATE FRONDS

B	R	E	T		U	R	I	S		S	T	I	L	L
R	O	A	R		P	A	N	T		E	R	N	I	E
I	N	R	E	A	L	I	T	Y		L	E	O	N	A
T	A	L	K	T	O	T	H	E	P	L	A	N	T	S
				H	A	T	E		R	E	D	E	Y	E
R	A	M	R	O	D		F	A	I	R				
I	L	I	U	M		K	I	L	N		E	D	G	E
I	V	E	N	E	V	E	R	S	T	U	D	I	E	D
S	A	N	G		I	N	S	O		B	E	N	N	Y
			S	P	O	T		R	A	N	G	E	S	
P	I	L	A	T	E		P	L	A	N				
A	N	Y	F	E	R	N	L	A	N	G	U	A	G	E
C	A	N	O	E		C	A	T	F	I	S	H	E	S
E	N	D	U	P		O	C	T	O		E	M	M	A
R	E	E	L	S		S	E	E	R		D	E	S	I

47 MORE OR LES

S	I	G	N		C	L	A	I	R		R	A	T	S
O	G	R	E		H	A	S	N	T		E	L	H	I
N	E	E	D	L	E	S	S	N	E	E	D	L	E	S
A	T	E		A	E	T	N	A		G	O	T	H	S
T	I	N	C	U	P		M	S	G		H	A	I	
A	T	E	A	R		P	E	E	P	S		E	V	E
			R	E	C	O	L	O	R		O	R	E	S
	N	A	P	L	E	S	S	N	A	P	L	E	S	
M	E	S	S		S	T	I	L	T	E	D			
A	A	S		C	A	S	E	Y		S	E	G	A	L
C	R	O		A	R	E		D	E	N	O	T	E	
A	B	N	E	R		A	P	A	R	T		A	R	N
B	E	A	T	L	E	S	S	B	E	A	T	L	E	S
R	E	N	T		K	O	A	L	A		V	I	S	E
E	R	T	E		E	N	T	E	R		S	E	T	S

65 SINGER'S RANGE

P	A	S	T	A		L	A	P	S		T	O	E	D
A	L	T	A	R		O	C	H	O		O	R	Z	O
N	O	R	S	E		A	E	O	N		P	E	R	I
T	H	A	T	T	E	N	D	T	O	B	F	L	A	T
S	A	W	Y	E	R	S		O	R	A	L			
			S	O	H	O		A	S	I	A	N	S	
W	A	I	F		D	A	N	K		I	G	L	O	O
I	N	O	R	D	E	R	T	O	C	S	H	A	R	P
E	N	N	U	I		K	A	R	A		T	W	A	S
N	O	S	I	N	G		P	E	R	M				
			T	A	R	A		A	L	A	B	A	M	A
W	H	I	C	H	I	S	A	N	A	T	U	R	A	L
H	E	R	A		S	H	O	W		T	R	E	N	T
I	M	O	K		L	E	N	A		E	R	A	S	E
Z	I	N	E		Y	S	E	R		D	O	S	E	R

12 ONE OF THE MAGNIFICENT SEVEN

D	A	Z	S	■	S	C	O	O	T	■	S	T	A	T
A	R	E	O	■	A	L	O	N	E	■	E	A	S	E
D	I	R	T	Y	D	O	Z	E	N	■	A	X	I	S
A	L	O	H	A	■	D	E	A	T	H	W	I	S	H
■	■	M	E	L	O	■	■	T	H	E	E	■	■	■
S	T	O	R	E	D	U	P	■	S	M	E	L	T	S
E	R	S	E	■	O	H	I	O	■	A	D	O	R	E
T	A	T	■	B	R	O	N	S	O	N	■	V	I	E
S	M	E	L	L	■	H	U	L	A	■	B	E	A	D
A	S	L	E	E	P	■	P	O	T	B	E	L	L	Y
■	■	N	E	R	O	■	■	H	A	L	E	■	■	■
S	A	N	D	P	I	P	E	R	■	B	U	T	T	E
O	N	C	E	■	M	R	M	A	J	E	S	T	Y	K
F	E	A	R	■	P	A	I	G	E	■	H	E	R	E
T	W	A	S	■	S	H	R	E	D	■	I	R	E	D

30 HI! DEFINITION

P	O	P	S	■	A	R	G	O	N	■	C	R	A	W
O	R	E	O	■	L	E	A	V	E	■	A	O	N	E
O	Z	O	N	E	L	A	Y	E	R	■	M	B	A	S
L	O	N	G	T	I	M	E	N	O	S	E	E	■	■
■	■	■	S	A	S	S	■	■	C	O	R	F	U	■
F	A	S	T	S	■	A	F	R	O	■	T	E	N	■
A	S	H	E	■	H	E	L	L	O	T	H	E	R	E
T	H	O	R	■	E	L	I	A	S	■	A	L	V	A
H	O	W	S	T	R	I	C	K	S	■	C	E	O	S
O	R	E	■	H	O	S	E	■	■	F	I	E	R	Y
M	E	R	G	E	■	■	A	L	E	E	■	■	■	■
■	G	O	O	D	A	F	T	E	R	N	O	O	N	■
T	R	I	O	■	A	C	E	B	A	N	D	A	G	E
R	U	F	F	■	F	R	E	A	K	■	A	T	R	A
A	T	T	Y	■	T	E	S	T	Y	■	S	H	E	L

48 LEAVING LAS VEGAS

L	O	W	E	■	A	C	H	E	■	C	H	A	M	P
A	L	E	X	■	B	R	A	Y	■	R	E	N	E	E
P	E	R	E	■	Y	O	R	E	■	A	R	N	A	Z
D	A	N	C	E	S	W	I	T	H	W	O	E	S	■
O	R	E	■	S	S	N	■	O	I	L	D	R	U	M
G	Y	R	O	S	■	S	H	O	T	S	■	I	R	A
■	■	T	E	M	■	E	T	S	■	A	C	E	D	■
■	C	A	I	N	A	N	D	H	O	B	B	E	S	■
E	R	R	S	■	N	A	G	■	N	I	B	■	■	■
L	E	M	■	C	A	M	E	O	■	P	A	N	D	A
M	A	C	H	O	N	E	■	R	T	E	■	O	R	R
■	T	H	O	M	A	S	A	A	E	D	I	S	O	N
S	U	A	V	E	■	A	R	T	E	■	N	O	P	E
P	R	I	E	D	■	K	E	E	N	■	D	A	I	S
F	E	R	R	Y	■	E	A	S	Y	■	O	P	T	S

66 YOU CAN SAY THAT AGAIN

T	I	G	E	■	S	A	F	I	R	E	■	S	T	A	T
A	N	O	N	■	P	R	I	D	E	S	■	U	H	U	H
I	D	O	L	■	L	O	S	E	I	T	■	D	I	N	O
■	A	D	A	M	A	N	T	A	D	A	M	A	N	T	■
I	N	D	I	E	S	■	■	■	T	O	N	S	I	L	■
A	G	E	■	W	H	O	C	A	R	E	S	■	K	E	Y
M	E	A	N	S	■	N	O	L	O	■	S	L	I	E	R
A	R	L	O	■	P	E	R	I	S	H	■	O	N	M	E
■	■	■	T	H	E	D	A	T	H	E	D	A	■	■	■
M	E	T	E	O	R	■	■	■	R	A	D	I	U	M	■
O	V	A	■	T	I	R	E	I	R	O	N	■	N	S	A
S	O	L	V	E	■	A	M	M	O	■	Z	O	N	E	D
A	L	K	A	L	I	N	E	A	L	K	A	L	I	N	E
I	V	E	S	■	T	I	N	G	L	Y	■	G	E	E	D
C	E	D	E	■	I	N	D	E	E	D	■	A	S	T	O

21 ART OF COMEDY

```
O M N I   T E R I   H I T M E
R O A M   O V E N   E L V I S
A T V S   L I N C   L I A R S
T H E O D D C O U P L E
E E L   R O T   S L O   B I G
D R O P I N   P T A   X E N A
    R A E   S O O N   E A T S
  H A R R Y A N D T O N T O
B O N K   E D D Y   N O S
Y O G A   M D S   R E N T A L
E K E   B E L   E O N   H U E
    H O N E Y M O O N E R S
X E R O X   B A A S   E R O S
K L I N E   A L I T   W A R E
E L M E R   G E L S   S P A R
```

39 SPECIFIC CONGRATS ...

```
O S L O   C R A G S   E D O M
S T A R   R E T R O   M I N D
U R S A   I N T O W   E N D S
  A T T A B O Y G E O R G E
V I S O R S     D A G A M A
I N T R O   T D S   R E L A X
D E R   D R Y R U N S   I N E
A R A L   I C A M E   I N D S
  W A Y T O G O L O N G
    Y E A     L U C
S E D A N   D I S   T H A N K
I M I N   C E N T S   A L O E
N I C E J O B S E C U R I T Y
E L E G A N T   W A R G A M E
W E D G I E S   S T E E R E D
```

57 THE END OF THE LINE

```
S E G A L   A M M O   A L E C
L A U R A   N O I R   B O N O
U T L E Y   I N N E R C I T Y
D E L T A   M E N S A   S R O
G R E E N B A Y     S P L A T
E S T   E E L   D E P L A N E
    P G A   B O P   A N T S
  R E G G I E W H I T E
S P E C   L T D   R N S
A R M O R E D   M O D   A G T
N O I S E   M I N I S T E R
J O N   E L I A S   A E T N A
O F D E F E N S E   I V I E D
S E E R   I G O R   N E R V E
E D D Y   F A N S   K N E A D
```

75 CONFLICT OF INTEREST

```
B E N T   S W A M I   U C L A
A D E E   O R L O N   T R O Y
E G O S   L I O N S S H A R E
R E N T S I T E   T H A M E S
  L E A D S   A R O N
F L I R T S   I N E R T S E T
A E G I S   E S T E E   H A I
K A H N   E R N S T   N O T E
E S T   A N N O Y   F E W E R
R E S E N T I T   P E T E R S
    I D E E   T O E R R
D I A L E R   T E N T I R E S
A C C E S S R O A D   T O R A
D E L E   I N U S E   E O N S
S T U N   T A T E R   S M E E
```

22 NATIONAL BORDERS

B	O	B	T	A	I	L	S		S	H	A	C	K	S
I	N	V	A	S	I	O	N		C	A	B	A	N	A
R	E	D	C	H	I	N	A	C	A	B	I	N	E	T
D	I	S	K				P	A	L	E	T	T	E	S
			L	A	R	S		B	E	A	M			
S	T	H	E	L	E	N	A			S	U	L	F	A
A	R	E		O	B	O	I	S	T		C	O	L	L
C	O	L	D	T	U	R	K	E	Y	S	H	O	O	T
H	U	G	E		S	T	E	P	P	E		I	W	O
S	T	A	R	S		N	I	E	L	S	E	N	S	
		A	P	S	E		A	B	L	E				
S	W	A	N	L	A	K	E			A	S	S	N	
H	A	N	G	I	N	G	C	H	A	D	L	O	W	E
I	N	T	E	N	T		C	A	R	O	U	S	E	S
N	E	E	D	T	O		E	P	I	C	P	O	E	T

40 VOCATIONS FOR DUMMIES

M	I	M	E	S		C	A	S	H		C	M	O	N
I	N	A	L	L		R	I	P	E		H	E	R	A
N	F	L	L	I	N	E	M	A	N		O	L	D	S
H	O	L	Y	C	O	W		S	H	E	R	B	E	T
			E	W	E	S		O	L	E	A	R	Y	
V	E	N	T	R	I	L	O	Q	U	I	S	T		
E	G	A	D	S		F	U	S	E		O	C	T	
T	A	M	S		E	S	T	E	E		D	A	L	I
O	N	E		B	R	I	E			R	O	S	I	E
		C	P	R	I	N	S	T	R	U	C	T	O	R
I	T	A	L	I	C		T	W	I	N				
M	I	L	I	T	I	A		I	P	A	N	E	M	A
A	B	L	E		D	R	E	S	S	M	A	K	E	R
G	E	E	R		L	I	S	T		O	V	E	R	T
E	R	R	S		E	A	T	S		K	E	S	E	Y

58 HO AND MO'

B	E	E	B		A	T	M	S		A	G	A	P	E
L	U	R	E		C	H	O	O		R	U	B	E	N
E	R	I	E		T	U	T	S		M	I	D	A	S
D	O	N	F	R	O	M	H	O	N	O	L	U	L	U
			S	E	R	B			O	R	E	L	S	E
P	A	S	T	A		N	I	M	O	Y				
E	T	H	E	L		A	S	I	S		S	M	O	G
C	R	E	A	M	F	I	L	L	E	D	C	A	K	E
S	A	L	K		A	L	E	E		E	A	T	A	T
			O	U	S	T	S		B	R	A	Y	S	
S	P	L	A	T	S			T	O	T	E			
L	A	U	G	H	T	E	R	O	F	S	A	N	T	A
O	P	I	N	E		D	A	N	A		W	O	O	L
W	A	G	E	R		G	R	E	G		A	L	O	T
S	W	I	S	S		E	A	S	E		Y	O	K	O

76 NAPOLEON BLOWN-APART

A	T	H	O	S		A	B	B	A		S	T	E	W
S	I	E	N	A		S	A	I	L		N	A	M	E
S	T	R	O	M		P	R	O	M		A	K	I	N
N	O	O	N	P	L	E	A		A	L	P	E	R	T
			E	L	A	N		S	N	O	O	T		
L	E	S	L	E	Y		L	E	A	P	N	O	N	O
A	Q	U	A		S	T	A	N	C	E		T	O	R
R	U	M	P	S		Y	T	D		S	P	A	R	S
V	I	M		A	S	S	I	S	I		E	S	S	O
A	P	E	O	N	L	O	N		S	U	N	K	E	N
		R	A	T	O	N		S	O	S	A			
P	I	C	K	A	T		P	O	N	E	L	O	A	N
E	T	A	L		C	O	O	N		D	O	D	G	E
R	I	M	E		A	R	O	N		U	N	D	E	R
I	S	P	Y		R	E	L	Y		P	O	S	E	D

13 GOT M-I-L-K?

```
C A L O R I E ■ S T O I C A L
S P A R E M E ■ A I R M A D A
A U N T I E O F D O R O T H Y
■ ■ D O N T ■ R E N ■ G E E ■
A C E ■ ■ ■ P A Y ■ P E R R Y
H U R R I C A N E C E N T E R
A R S E N A L ■ D R S ■ O D S
■ ■ X V I ■ ■ ■ A E F ■ ■ ■
A D A ■ A R I ■ L I T E R A L
F A S H I O N M A G A Z I N E
T Y S O N ■ S E X ■ ■ S A X ■
■ C E L ■ P T A ■ B O N E ■ ■
B A N D L E A D E R K Y S E R
A R T I E S T ■ L E I S U R E
T E S T A T E ■ S W E E P E A
```

31 TRANSIT BENEATH

```
C D S ■ S U M U P ■ S E T T O
H O C ■ C R E P E ■ A C H E D
A N I ■ U N D E R G R O U N D
I N F E R ■ I N K E D ■ M D S
R A I L R O A D ■ T O M B ■ ■
■ ■ ■ F Y I ■ B A N A N A S
A H A ■ L A T E ■ I T A L L
S U B W A Y F R A N C H I S E
I N N E R ■ T U T U ■ L O W
S T E R E O S ■ ■ M P S ■ ■
■ G E A R ■ T U B E T O P S
O N A ■ C E D E S ■ L A L A W
M E T R O S E X U A L ■ O W E
A H E A D ■ L A R G E ■ R E P
R I D G E ■ A S Y E T ■ D D T
```

49 SOLE MUSIC

```
R A M A ■ S E T T O ■ E B A N
O R E L ■ E T A I L ■ N I L E
G E N E P I T N E Y ■ S L O W
E N D W I S E ■ A M P U L E S
T A O I S M ■ ■ P R E Y ■ ■
■ ■ V A I N ■ T I A ■ J F K
E L B E ■ C O N W A Y ■ O L A
G U E S S ■ T A I ■ S P E A R
A K A ■ T W I T T Y ■ I L K A
D E C ■ E I N ■ S O N G ■ ■
■ H E E L ■ ■ R E L I V E
R O B A R D S ■ S K I A R E A
P L O T ■ C A R P E N T E R S
M A Y A ■ A L T A R ■ I N G E
S Y S T ■ T E E M S ■ N E E D
```

67 WHAT HAPPENED WHEN ...

```
V A P I D ■ V I C I ■ T O A T
A B A T E ■ I C O N ■ I O W A
C U S T E R C U S S E D H E R
S T A Y P U T ■ M E L I S S A
■ ■ ■ S H I M ■ A V E ■ ■
M I S T E R M I S S E D H E R
O M A H A ■ N E O S ■ E L I
P E S O ■ F E I G N ■ B A L D
U T E ■ D I S C ■ K A T I E
P A S T O R P A S S E D H E R
■ ■ O N E ■ M U O N ■ ■ ■
A L U M N A E ■ N A N E T T E
B U S T E R B U S S E D H E R
I N S O ■ M A Z E ■ T I A R A
T E R M ■ S N I T ■ H E I R S
```

14 FIVE SIMPLE WAYS TO REMEMBER JOHN RITTER

32 SIZE MATTERS

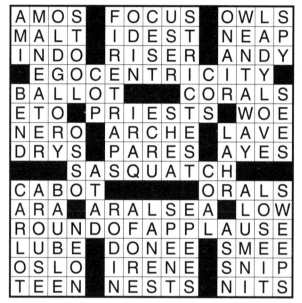

50 FLIP-FLOP

68 WITH A HEAVY HEART

23 PASS THE TATERS

```
B A S I L ■ C H I C ■ C A S E
O C O M E ■ A U T O ■ A R T Y
S N U F F Y S M I T H S K I D
H E R ■ T A K E ■ T A H I N I
■ ■ C O W L S ■ L O Z E N G E
B I R D I E ■ G E N E S ■ ■
A T E I N ■ B O A T ■ G O O
S L A N G F O R H O M E R U N
E L M ■ O R G Y ■ E R A S E
■ ■ G A U G E ■ F A I N T S
L A S A L L E ■ T O T E D ■
O U T I E S ■ O R E L ■ P A W
F R E N C H F R Y S O U R C E
T A L E ■ O U Z O ■ A P I L E
Y S E R ■ T R O N ■ F I X U P
```

41 SWITCH POSITIONS

```
O M I T ■ D I S K S ■ B R I T
R I D E ■ E L L I E ■ E U R O
A S T A ■ L E A R N ■ E N V Y
C H A S T I T Y B O F F O ■
L A G E R ■ ■ S Y R A C U S E
E P S T E I N ■ S T A T E N
■ ■ E T A I L ■ ■ K O N G
■ F O R D A Y S O F F E N D
H O K E ■ ■ S H O A L ■ ■
M I L S A P ■ T R U D G E S
M E A T L O A F ■ F O U N T
■ H O L I D A Y O F F I C E
O D O R ■ R O B E D ■ F L O W
N A M E ■ O B E S E ■ E T R E
S H A D ■ T E R M S ■ D Y E D
```

59 ARTICLE REWRITTEN

```
E A R P ■ M E C C A ■ E C C E
G L E E ■ E T H O S ■ X O U T
A L F A ■ A T O M S ■ P R E S
D O E S A N U M B E R O N ■
S T R I C T ■ P O S E ■ F E M
■ ■ N E I L ■ S A F I R E
A N E A R M I S S ■ D R E A D
G U L P ■ E M I T S ■ E L S E
I D I O M ■ A N E A T I D E A
L E A D E N ■ P R I G ■ ■
E S S ■ R I S K ■ A D H E R E
■ H A V E A N I C E T R I P
A T O P ■ C L O S E ■ C O P E
R O W E ■ E L L E N ■ A D U E
T R E X ■ S E L E S ■ R E P S
```

77 I ONLY HAVE I'S FOR YOU

```
L I S Z T ■ K I S S ■ S I M I
I N H I S ■ I R I S ■ K N I T
F R I G H T W I G S ■ I F N I
T I P ■ I W I S H ■ S P I T S
■ ■ T R I S H ■ S W I G S
P R I N T S ■ S M I T H ■ ■
H I N T ■ T H R I L L ■ T V S
D I D S T ■ I I S ■ L X I I I
S S I ■ R I S K I T ■ I N D C
■ S N I T S ■ H I N G I S
■ S T I N T ■ I S I N G ■ ■
B L I N I ■ S T I R S ■ K I M
L I N T ■ S K I N D I V I N G
I T C H ■ D I S K ■ S C R I M
P S T S ■ I S I S ■ T R I T T
```

24 GIRL, INTERRUPTED

V	C	H	I	P		H	A	M	M		O	W	L	S
E	R	O	D	E		O	D	I	E		C	H	A	T
L	A	T	I	N	C	R	O	S	S		C	O	T	Y
O	N	B	O	A	R	D		C	H	A	U	C	E	R
U	K	E			Y	E	A	H		G	R	A	P	E
R	Y	D	E	R		S	L	I	C	E		R	A	N
		R	E	P		L	E	O		L	E	S	E	
	L	E	A	V	E	S	O	F	G	R	A	S	S	
S	A	S	S		N	O	V		S	O	S			
C	S	T		I	N	F	E	R		T	S	A	R	S
E	V	I	C	T		T	R	U	E			G	E	E
N	E	M	E	S	E	S		B	A	S	E	H	I	T
E	G	A	D		L	O	W	E	R	C	L	A	S	S
R	A	T	A		M	A	I	N		A	S	S	E	T
Y	S	E	R		O	P	T	S		M	E	T	R	O

42 GO WASH OUT YOUR MOUTH!

P	A	T	S		C	A	C	T	I		T	O	R	I
O	M	I	T		S	C	O	O	T		O	V	E	N
L	I	P	R	E	A	D	E	R	S		G	E	N	A
A	N	T	E	S		C	U	S	S	W	O	R	D	S
R	O	O	S	T	S		R	O	O	K		T	E	E
	R	E	S	E	N	T				S	C	O	R	N
		T	R	A	I	P	S	E		O	N	E	S	
W	A	L	E		R	E	D	O	X		M	E	R	E
O	N	U	S		E	A	T	H	E	R	E			
R	A	T	T	Y			O	C	E	A	N	S		
N	T	H		E	L	I	S		S	T	R	A	T	A
T	H	E	Y	W	A	T	C	H		R	O	S	E	S
H	E	R	O		W	H	A	T	Y	O	U	S	A	Y
I	M	A	Y		N	O	L	T	E			N	A	M	E
N	A	N	O		S	T	E	P	S		D	U	S	T

60 EMPLOYEE-EMPLOYER
RELATIONSHIP

W	A	S	P	S		D	O	G	S		C	R	U	Z
I	F	E	E	L		I	C	O	N		A	H	M	E
L	O	L	L	Y		S	H	O	U	T	D	O	W	N
C	O	F	F	E	E	C	O	F	F	E	R			
O	T	C		S	A	S			F	R	E	N	C	H
		O	A	T	S		O	W	L	S		U	R	E
Z	I	N	G		E	S	T	E	E	E	S	T	E	R
A	C	T	E	D		H	E	R		R	A	C	E	D
P	A	R	E	E	P	A	R	E	R		I	R	K	S
P	L	O		M	E	D	I		O	L	L	A		
A	L	L	W	E	T		G	R	E		C	D	T	
		Y	A	N	K	E	E	Y	A	N	K	E	R	
G	O	B	A	N	A	N	A	S		N	E	E	D	Y
I	B	E	T		M	I	S	T		T	I	R	E	S
L	I	N	T		E	T	T	E		O	N	S	E	T

78 THEMELESS CHALLENGER

T	I	B	E	T		S	P	A	R		B	E	D	S
A	M	A	T	I		T	E	L	E	G	E	N	I	C
S	O	R	T	A		E	N	T	E	R	I	N	T	O
T	U	B	E	R		A	C	E	S	A	T	E	S	T
E	T	A		A	D	M	I	R	E	S				
	A	R	A		A	I	L		S	P	A	R	T	A
P	H	A	T		N	E	S	T		S	M	U	R	F
L	E	A	R		O	S	H	E	A		O	M	A	R
E	R	N	E	S		T	A	N	S		N	O	V	O
A	E	N	E	A	S		R	T	E		G	R	E	
			L	E	A	P	D	A	Y		M	L	B	
I	N	A	C	O	R	N	E	R		E	L	I	D	E
G	A	S	E	N	G	I	N	E		S	O	L	A	R
O	P	P	O	S	I	T	E	S		N	O	L	T	E
T	E	S	S		O	A	R	S		O	N	S	E	T

15 CRAZY PEOPLE ARE WHAT THEY EAT

```
J I B E   E M I T   A T O Z
A L E X   D A R E   T H A I
R E A P   I N O N   R I F T
    T O P B A N A N A S
A P E   E L N I N O   M E S
S A N   R E A C T S   I D I
T Y P E O       E R N I E
H E A L T H F O O D N U T S
M E T S   E T O N   S T E T
A S H   O L D P R O   E D A
      A W L     E A R
    S A F E C R A C K E R S
P U L L   A U T O   S E A T
E R M A   T S A R   E A S E
Z E S T   S E N D   T R E X
```

33 DATA BANCROFT

```
C A L L S   E L B A   L I Z A
A L E U T   S O U R   O N E S
N A A C P   A L I T   S U N K
A N N I E S U L L I V A N
L I E D T O     T S E L I O T
S S R   E L S A   T E A S E R
      B R A H M A   M O D E
    M R S R O B I N S O N
K N E E   R E D O E S
E S S A Y S   R A T E   O B S
G A S K E T S     E S C R O W
    M A R Y M A G D A L E N E
D R A W   M A L E   W I L E D
R I T A   I R O N   E N S U E
J O E Y   E T T A   D E E P S
```

51 YOUR SOMETHING ELSE

```
A W A C S   S O R B   C L O P
R E C A P   O A H U   H O U R
G A R B O   U T E S   A W R Y
O N E S T A R H O T E L S
      T A G S   I N K P A D
  D O G E A R   S N O   I T I
P A R I S   A C C T   A R O N
O N E S T O P S H O P P I N G
S C O T   V E T O   O S T E O
E E C   W E S   O G R E S S
D R O V E R   P L A T
    O N E S T O R Y H O U S E
J O K E   H A L O   O W N E R
E R I C   O L E O   L E T A T
T R E K   T E R M   E N O T E
```

69 TWO WEEKS' NOTICE

```
M A M A   A R S O N   T B S P
A V O N   S E E M E   H O A R
D O N E   T A R O T   A B L Y
A W K W A R D B O W K N O T
M A E   P O E   E Y E L I D
E L Y S E   R A B I D   I N E
    E E L   R I G   K N E W
  L O W K E Y M O H A W K S
P O P S   G E E   T E A
E V E   D A N D Y   I N A W E
C E R E A L   E S O   T O N
  M A W K I S H S Q U A W K S
P E T E   S H A M U   L I E U
O D O R   M E D E A   F L U E
T O R S   S L A N T   A L P S
```

16 FIRST OF THE MONTH

B	O	C	A	■	D	E	B	R	A	■	E	N	V	S
A	P	A	R	■	I	M	E	A	N	■	M	E	N	U
S	E	P	T	I	C	T	A	N	K	■	U	S	E	R
E	N	G	I	N	E	S	■	U	A	R	■	T	C	M
P	A	U	S	E	■	■	A	P	R	E	S	S	K	I
A	I	N	T	■	U	S	N	■	A	L	L	I	E	S
Y	R	S	■	T	R	I	A	D	■	A	A	N	D	E
■	■	■	J	U	N	G	L	E	G	Y	M	■	■	■
R	E	H	A	B	■	H	Y	M	N	S	■	V	A	T
U	R	A	N	U	S	■	S	O	P	■	W	A	C	O
N	O	V	E	L	I	S	T	■	C	O	L	O	N	■
I	S	E	■	E	T	C	■	A	S	A	R	U	L	E
N	I	N	A	■	T	H	I	R	T	Y	D	A	Y	S
T	O	O	T	■	E	M	O	T	E	■	E	T	T	U
O	N	T	V	■	R	O	U	E	N	■	D	E	E	P

34 BACK AND FORTH

I	C	E	T	■	O	W	E	S	■	A	S	P	I	E
T	O	R	O	■	R	O	R	Y	■	S	T	U	N	T
S	C	R	A	P	I	R	O	N	■	E	A	T	A	T
M	O	O	D	O	F	D	O	O	M	■	R	A	C	E
E	A	R	■	P	I	G	■	D	E	S	O	T	O	■
■	■	O	S	C	A	R	■	W	A	F	E	R	S	■
C	L	E	M	■	E	M	I	R	■	C	R	A	N	E
H	O	M	E	■	S	E	V	E	R	■	A	S	E	A
I	C	O	N	S	■	S	A	T	E	■	T	E	R	M
P	A	T	O	I	S	■	L	I	A	R	S	■	■	■
■	L	I	F	T	E	D	■	C	S	I	■	A	S	I
E	C	O	N	■	M	A	D	E	O	F	E	D	A	M
L	A	N	E	S	■	M	I	N	N	E	S	O	T	A
L	L	A	M	A	■	E	C	C	E	■	P	R	I	M
A	L	L	O	W	■	S	E	E	R	■	O	N	E	S

52 SO TO SPEEK

U	R	S	A	■	O	G	L	E	S	■	I	M	U	S
P	E	W	S	■	B	E	I	G	E	■	R	I	N	K
P	E	E	K	P	E	R	F	O	R	M	A	N	C	E
E	V	A	■	A	R	M	E	N	I	A	■	I	L	E
R	E	T	A	I	L	■	■	A	L	L	S	E	T	■
■	S	P	R	I	N	G	A	L	E	E	K	■	■	■
S	O	H	O	■	N	I	E	L	S	■	A	I	L	S
W	H	I	P	S	■	E	E	L	■	A	P	R	I	L
A	I	R	■	T	I	C	K	O	F	F	■	T	E	A
N	O	T	A	O	N	E	■	T	A	L	K	S	U	P
■	■	■	G	R	R	■	J	A	I	■	■	■	■	■
■	W	E	E	K	A	S	A	K	I	T	T	E	N	■
G	O	G	O	■	N	I	P	A	T	■	S	U	E	Z
A	R	A	L	■	G	R	E	T	A	■	C	R	O	P
R	E	D	D	■	E	S	S	E	S	■	H	O	N	G

70 COLLATERAL DAMAGE

A	S	S	N	■	R	E	B	U	S	■	A	M	F	M
P	A	L	O	■	E	X	U	L	T	■	W	E	R	E
P	R	O	V	■	M	I	L	N	E	■	A	R	E	A
L	A	T	E	C	O	L	L	A	R	■	I	C	E	T
E	N	S	L	A	V	E	■	N	A	T	I	V	E	■
■	■	■	I	R	A	■	S	H	A	D	■	L	E	A
S	P	E	D	■	L	O	C	A	L	A	L	E	R	T
T	I	N	E	S	■	P	A	R	■	M	A	S	S	E
R	E	C	A	L	L	A	L	T	O	■	U	S	E	R
A	C	H	■	O	I	L	Y	■	R	I	G	■	■	■
T	E	A	S	E	T	■	B	I	S	H	O	P	S	■
E	R	N	E	■	T	A	L	L	O	R	A	C	L	E
G	A	T	E	■	E	Q	U	A	L	■	B	E	A	N
I	T	E	M	■	R	U	S	S	E	■	L	A	I	D
C	E	D	E	■	S	A	T	E	S	■	E	N	D	S